I0233819

HOMO AMOR

AND

UNIQUE SELF

HOMO AMOR

AND

UNIQUE SELF

. . .

A Revolutionary Path Towards

A Planetary Awakening In Love

Through Unique Self Symphonies

One Mountain, Many Paths: Oral Essays
Volume 22

DR. MARC GAFNI AND
BARBARA MARX HUBBARD

Copyright © 2025 Center for World Philosophy and Religion

All Rights Reserved

No part of this book may be used or reproduced in any manner whatsoever without written permission except in the case of brief quotations embodied in critical articles or reviews.

No part of this book may be reproduced, or stored in a retrieval system, or transmitted in any form or by any means, electronic, mechanical, photocopying, recording, or otherwise, without express written permission of the publisher.

All brand names and product names used in this book are trademarks, registered trademarks, or trade names of their respective holders.

For additional information and press releases please contact CWPR Publishing.

Author: Marc Gafni and Barbara Marx Hubbard
Title: Homo Amor & Unique Self
Identifiers: ISBN 979-8-88834-032-5 (electronic)
ISBN 979-8–88834–031–8 (paperback)

© 2025 Marc Gafni

Edited by Kathy Brownback, Talya Bloom, and Elena Maslova-Levin

World Philosophy and Religion Press,
St. Johnsbury, VT
in conjunction with

IP Integral Publishers

https://worldphilosophyandreligion.org

CONTENTS

CHAPTER 4   EVERY PLACE I'VE BEEN I NEEDED TO BE

CHAPTER 5   CONFESS YOUR BROKENNESS; CONFESS YOUR GREATNESS

CHAPTER 12   WHAT'S MISSING FROM CULTURE: A MODEL OF SELF—ANSWERING THE QUESTION, "WHO AM I?"

CHAPTER 13   THE DIVINE DELIGHT AND DEVASTATION OF
              DEVOTION AND HER DIGNITIES: VISIONS OF
              UNIQUE SELF AND UNIQUE SELF SYMPHONY

EDITORIAL NOTE ABOUT AUTHORSHIP, EDITING, AND THE RADICAL CONTEXT FOR THIS SERIES

ORAL ESSAYS FROM THE ONE MOUNTAIN, MANY PATHS WEEKLY BROADCAST

This volume is part of the Oral Essays library, a series of lightly edited, compiled transcripts of oral teachings given by Dr. Marc Gafni and the late Barbara Marx Hubbard in their weekly online broadcast, *One Mountain, Many Paths,* which they co-founded in 2017. Originally called an "Evolutionary Church," *One Mountain, Many Paths* became a key venue for the articulation of an inspired and deeply grounded new Story of Value in response to the meta-crisis. Marc and Barbara—together with Zak Stein,[1] Kristina Kincaid, Ken Wilber, Sally Kempton, Lori Galperin, Aubrey Marcus and dozens of other thought-leaders over the years—began to articulate what they call a World Philosophy and World Religion[2] as a context for our diversity.

---

1 Zak, together with Ken Wilber, has been Marc's primary intellectual partner and an initiate lineage holder in CosmoErotic Humanism.

2 This project is grounded in four core organizational frameworks: 1) The Center for World Philosophy and Religion, co-founded by Marc Gafni, Zachary Stein, Sally Kempton, and Ken Wilber, and chaired over the years by John P. Mackey, Barbara Marx Hubbard, Aubrey Marcus, Gabrielle Anwar and Shareef Malnik, Carrie Kish and Adam Bellow, and Kathleen J. Brownback. 2) The Office for the Future, chaired by Stephanie Valcke and Ivan Bossyut. 3) The World Philosophy and Religion Press, founded and chaired by Aubrey Marcus, together with Marc Gafni and Zachary Stein. 4) The Foundation for Conscious Evolution, founded by Barbara Marx Hubbard and currently chaired by Peter Fiekowsky. For a complete list of key leadership, see the Office for the Future website, www.officeforthefuture.com.

Until Barbara's passing in 2019, she and Marc transmitted teachings together as evolutionary partners and "whole mates," weaving together insights and transmissions from their decades of practice, study, teaching, and activism into a synergy of wisdom, a grounded vision for future policy across all sectors of society.

Much of the *dharma* material below comes directly from Marc, so it was originally all in quotation marks—but that looked a little odd. So per his suggestion we removed them, and the reader should consider the paragraphs on the next several pages as one extended quote from him. We are joyfully grateful to Marc for the clarity of his *dharma*, the elegance and "second simplicity" of this language, and the mad, Outrageous Love with which he transmits his teachings.

Barbara and Marc called the mission of *One Mountain* "a Planetary Awakening in Evolutionary Love Through Unique Self Symphonies." We are an evolutionary community with a deeply grounded, radically alive, and "post-tragic" revolutionary spirit. We are activating a new humanity and awakening as a new species: *Homo amor*, the fulfillment of *Homo sapiens*.

One Mountain is committed to articulating a Story of Value that can become the ground for the new society that must be birthed in response to the meta-crisis. We recognize that we are living at a pivotal moment in history. In this "time between stories," the great moral imperative is to tell the new Story of Value. It is ours to do, personally and collectively, with great trembling and ecstatic joy.

FROM DOGMA TO DHARMA: ETERNAL AND EVOLVING FIRST PRINCIPLES AND FIRST VALUES

The teachings are grounded in decades of deep study across many wisdom traditions. Over the years, week by week, these teachings were incrementally developed within the framework of the *One Mountain, Many Paths* broadcast. We often refer to these teachings as *dharma*.

This word was originally used in lineage traditions to refer to something like universal law. This is a crucial realization: just as there is universal law in mathematical value, there is also a sense of universal law in ethics and value.

Historically, *dharma* often devolved into unchanging dogma. Evolution was ignored, and the natural process of *dharma* evolution became disconnected from its deep, eternal context. The weakness of the word *dharma* is that too often it did not include the evolving insights of the sciences, it confused local cultural truths with universal truths, and it used words like "eternal," as in "eternal Tao," as opposed to words like "evolution."

Eternal came to mean unchanging, and that kind of thinking often led to overly ethnocentric readings of *dharma*. Local systems would claim their religious and cultural insights as immutable, which stood in the way of the emergence of a genuine world Story of Value that is real, inherent to Cosmos, and backed by the Universe—even as it is also always evolving.

Or, as we often say, "eternal value is evolving value. The eternal Tao is the evolving Tao."

We have shown that, emergent from profound insights in the "interior sciences," eternal does not mean unchanging in time; it means what we call the deeper Field of ErosValue that is beneath culture, geography, and history, which lives beneath all individual and collective values, and beneath time and space itself.

As such, we have gradually transitioned from the term *dharma* to the term *Value*, in the sense of the Field of Value that lives beneath all values. This Field of Value discloses as First Principles and First Values embedded in a Story of Value.

Indeed, as the interior sciences knew and the exterior sciences imply, Reality arises in a Field of ErosValue in which an entire set of mathematical, musical, molecular, moral, and mystical values are the very ground of all being. That Field of Value is eternal—the true ground of the Good, True and Beautiful—even as it is evolving.

But of course, it is equally critical not just to talk about evolving value, but to ground the evolving value in its true nature, the eternal Field of First Principles and First Values, always reaching for ever more life, ever more love, ever more care, ever more depth, ever more uniqueness, ever more intimate communion, and ever more transformation.

As such, when we refer to the word *dharma*, which still appears in these texts together with the word value, we refer to an evolving *dharma* grounded in an *eternal and evolving* Field of Value. Indeed, eternity and evolution are two faces of the whole, opposites joined at the hip, that characterize the nature of our Cosmos in virtually all of its expressions.

It's in these terms that we ground a robust world philosophy that integrates the validated, leading-edge insights of premodern traditional wisdom, modern wisdom, and more recent postmodern insights, weaving them together into a new whole greater than the sum of its parts.

This new whole is a shared Story of Value rooted in First Principles and First Values that are both eternal and evolving.

These First Principles and First Values of Cosmos are woven together into a new Story of Value as a context for our diversity, a new Universe Story. This new story gives us the best possible responses we have to the mystery, and to the great questions:

- Who am I? Who are we?
- Where am I? Where are we?
- What should I do? What should we do?

It is only through such a shared Universe Story—a narrative of identity and ethos as a context for our blessed diversity—that we can realize how what unites us is so much greater than what divides us.

Only a new Story of Value will allow us to both respond to the meta-crisis and participate together in birthing the most true, good, and beautiful world that we already know is possible.

THIS ORAL ESSAYS SERIES IS AN ENTRYWAY TO THE GREAT LIBRARY OF COSMOEROTIC HUMANISM

This Oral Essays series is part of the overarching project of the Great Library at the Center for World Philosophy and Religion, led by Dr. Marc Gafni, together with Dr. Zak Stein. The aim of the Great Library project is to articulate a robust and comprehensive new Story of Value, CosmoErotic Humanism, in the form of dozens of well-researched and extensively footnoted academic works.

Our vision is to provide the philosophical framework that will be vital for navigating humanity through this time of immense crisis and transformation.

To begin your journey into CosmoErotic Humanism, we tenderly refer you to the book *First Principles and First Values*, co-authored by Marc Gafni, Zak Stein, and Ken Wilber, under the name David J. Temple. David J. Temple is a pseudonym created for enabling ongoing collaborative authorship at the Center for World Philosophy and Religion. The two primary authors behind David J. Temple are Marc Gafni and Zak Stein, and for different projects, specific writers will be named as part of the collaboration, such as Ken Wilber and others.

Three other volumes complete this introduction: *A Return to Eros*, by Marc Gafni and Kristina Kincaid; *Your Unique Self*, by Marc Gafni; and *Education in a Time between Worlds*, by Zak Stein.

We hope that the Oral Essays in the present volume, with their informal style of transmission, will serve as an allurement and entryway for you into the more formal books of the Great Library that provide the robust intellectual underpinnings of the new Story of Value.

A NOTE ABOUT THE EDITORS

This Oral Essays collection has been edited by students of the new Story of CosmoErotic Humanism. Each of us has actively participated in *One Mountain, Many Paths,* and most of us have been in deep "Holy of Holies" study with Dr. Marc Gafni for many years.

We have been privileged to find ourselves well-versed in the teachings, and even emerging as lineage-holders of CosmoErotic Humanism.[3]

We view this editing project as a privilege and a deep practice of study and clarification. We experience ourselves as a *mystical editing society,* frequently meeting and conversing together about the content—the depth of knowledge and wisdom offered here—as well as the technical intricacies involved with publishing a beautiful and coherent series of books. In so

---

3   CosmoErotic Humanism is a world philosophical movement aimed at reconstructing the collapse of value at the core of global culture. Much like Romanticism or Existentialism, CosmoErotic Humanism is not merely a theory but a movement that changes the very mood of Reality. It is an invitation to participate in evolving the source code of consciousness and culture towards a cosmocentric *ethos* for a planetary civilization.

The term CosmoErotic Humanism, initially coined by Dr. Gafni and colleagues, points to a complex, multi-faceted, layered, and nuanced evolutionary set of insights that has evolved over decades of intensive research, teaching, and spiritual practice from deep within a wide range of wisdom traditions (including the Wisdom of Solomon lineage tradition, Bodhisattva Buddhism, and Kashmir Shaivism), as well as multiple disciplines including complexity theory, chaos theory, emergence theory, molecular biology, and the more classical disciplines of the humanities.

The seeds of CosmoErotic Humanism were planted with Dr. Marc Gafni's work on a two-volume, 1,000-page opus called *Radical Kabbalah* (Integral Publishers, 2012). This scholarly work, sourced from deep study within the esoteric lineage texts of the Wisdom of Solomon, points to a non-dual, or acosmic, realization which—unlike the prevailing conceptualization of non-duality—does not efface the human being; rather, it is highly humanistic in its nature. The next step in the evolution of CosmoErotic Humanism was the insight that all of Reality is evolving Eros, which lives in, as, and through the human being.

A failure of Eros leads inexorably to the creation of narratives of "pseudo-eros." CosmoErotic Humanism is a response to the modern mental and social breakdown sourced in the proliferation of multiple forms of pseudo-eros and its broken narratives, such as rivalrous conflict governed by win/lose metrics and the dogmatic denial of intrinsic value in Cosmos, which together generate our current "global intimacy disorder."

doing, we function as a "Unique Self Symphony," which itself is a *dharmic* term that connotes an omni-considerate collaboration between realized Unique Selves synergizing our unique gifts into a new emergence greater than the sum of the parts. Even as we worked diligently to standardize our editing styles, meeting on a weekly basis to debate the nuances of phrasing, we also operated from within a deep appreciation of the unique style that each editor brought to his or her work. As such, the reader might notice some variation in editing style among the books.

Please note that Dr. Marc Gafni has not reviewed these edited Oral Essays, as he is deeply engaged in writing the formal books of the Great Library. But he has been generous in responding to questions and providing overall guidance in the project. Overall, as Marc's students and students of the *dharma*, we have made it a key project at the Center to publish these pieces of work relatively independently.

OUR UNIQUE ORAL-ESSAY EDITING STYLE PRESERVES THE ENERGY OF THE ORIGINAL TRANSMISSION

Dr. Marc Gafni is a uniquely gifted teacher whose oral transmission is imbued with a quality that has proven transformative for his students. Many of us feel mystically transformed by both the content and the underlying energy of the transmission style. Therefore, as we like to say, *trust the magic ways the dharma comes through your unique understanding!*

As Marc's empowered students, colleagues, and beloved friends, we have a deep knowing that these teachings are vital for the survival and thriving of humanity as we know it, and we recognize the importance of publishing his teachings in a written format that will be accessible by future generations. At the same time, we sought to preserve the Eros of the original oral transmission with all of its nuance, power, and depth. Our intention in the editing process, to the greatest extent possible, has been to keep these spoken artifacts intact in order to maintain the flow of the original transmission. We have therefore chosen not to engage in intensive formal editing, as we found that doing so resulted in the loss of the energetic transmission that is so key to fully receiving the *dharma*.

After experimenting with many ways to present these texts, we developed a specific way of laying out the text on the page. Marc, in collaboration with Zak Stein and Russian intellectual/artist Elena Maslova-Levin—and ultimately all of the editors, through many conversations—developed a unique, artistic presentation of the text, using bolding, italics, bullet points, and other stylistic features which together serve to accentuate the immediacy of the oral transmission.

As part of this editing style, intended to preserve the integrity of the original transmission, we have refrained from removing the frequent recapitulations of key themes. We found that each recapitulation contributes something vital to the rhythm and music beneath the words, like the beating drum of our hearts. These recapitulations not only review previous material but also add important new emphases, perspectives, and elements of the new Story of Value. We ask for your patience as a reader to trust the rhythm of these texts, and we trust you as a reader to have the depth and steadiness to find your way through.

KEY COMPONENTS: LINK TO THE ORIGINAL BROADCAST, EVOLUTIONARY LOVE CODES AND PRAYER

To supplement the written word, each episode includes a QR code linking to the original broadcast on YouTube, as well as occasional links to featured songs and video clips.

Each episode also centers around an "Evolutionary Love Code," formulated by Marc. These codes are part of the ongoing articulation and distillation of the *dharma* as it unfolds and emerges, week by week, over the course of many years, through the mystical process we call Outrageous Love or Evolutionary Love.

Another core component of the *One Mountain, Many Paths* episodes is what Marc and Barbara called "Evolutionary Prayer." Prayer is experienced in *One Mountain* not in the old fundamentalist sense of a "cosmic vending-machine god" who is alienated from Cosmos. Marc refers to this as the "god you do not and should not believe in"—and he often adds, "the god you don't believe in does not exist."

GOD IS THE INFINITE INTIMATE

In fact, in the *dharma* of CosmoErotic Humanism, a new name for God has emerged: the "Infinite Intimate," who appears in first-, second-, and third-person expressions. Marc first shared this name as he heard it whispered in 2023, although earlier intimations and formulations of the name appeared as early as 2010.

In first person, God is infinitely alive and as intimate as our own first-person experience.

In second person, God is the infinitely intimate Personhood of Cosmos that knows our name and holds us—the God about whom we say, *whenever we fall, we fall into Her hands*. This is the God who is our Beloved, Father, Mother, Lover, and Evolutionary Partner.

Finally, in third person, God inheres in all of the First Principles and First Values of Cosmos, and in the laws of science (both interior and exterior) that govern manifest Reality.

Therefore, we have a realization of God as not only the Infinity of Power but also the Infinity of Intimacy.

In *One Mountain, Many Paths*, we are reclaiming prayer at a higher level of consciousness. And we are reclaiming prayer as deep, alive, loving, and intimate conversations with God as the Infinite Intimate who knows our name.

THE INVITATION

We invite you to find your way into this revolution. Each one of our Unique Selves and unique gifts are desperately needed as we co-create this new Story of Value together, as part of the covenant between generations, for the sake of the whole.

Let's *play a larger game* and evolve the very source code of consciousness and culture together.

With mad love,

The Editors

LOVE OR DIE

LOCATING OURSELVES: ARTICULATING THE ESSENTIAL CONTEXT FOR THE ONE MOUNTAIN, MANY PATHS ORAL ESSAYS

SETTING OUR INTENTION

Intention setting is everything.

We're here—as da Vinci was with his cohort in the Renaissance—**to play a larger game, to participate in the evolution of love, which is to tell the new Story of Value rooted in First Principles and First Values.**

- Our intention is to recognize the critical historical juncture in which we find ourselves.
- Our intention is to take our seat at the table of history and to say, *we take responsibility for this.*
- Our intention is to participate as revolutionaries for the sake of the whole.

What we're here to do is revolution; revolution for the sake of the evolution of love.

It's a revolution for the sake of the trillions of unborn lives that will not manifest:

- The unborn loves
- The unborn creativity
- The unborn goodness
- The unborn truth
- The unborn beauty

All of it looks to us.

Not because we're engaged in grandiosity. Not at all!

- We're trembling before She.
- We're trembling with joy at the privilege.
- We're trembling with joy at the responsibility.
- We're trembling with joy at the Possibility of Possibility.
- We have to enact a new story in this moment of time. Because it is only a new story that can change the vector of history.

The most revolutionary act that we can do—the greatest moral imperative of this time—**is to articulate a new story at this time between worlds and this time between stories**.

Story is not made up, as postmodernity suggests. **We all live in inescapable frameworks; our framework is the story we live in.** Right now, Reality lives according to win/lose metrics, a story that is generating existential risk. **We need to change that story.**

When we change that story, when we tell a new story—not a made-up story, but a new Story of Value, rooted in First Principles and First Values—**then it all changes.**

We need to participate in the evolution of the source code of consciousness and culture, which is the evolution of love.

It's the most important, exciting, evolutionary, revolutionary act that we can do to alleviate suffering: to be lovers.

Like Rumi, the great poet of Sufism, we have to be "mad lovers," because it's the only sanity.

To be mad lovers is to see around the corner, to not be so obsessed with the details of the contractions of my life.

Let me see bigger.

Let me take complete care of myself in every possible way, let me completely attend to those in my circle of intimacy and influence, and then—*let me expand my circle.*

That's what we're here for.

- ◆ Our intention is to participate in the *LoveForce*, the *LoveIntelligence*, the *LoveBeauty*, the *LoveDesire* that literally animates Cosmos all the way up and all the way down.
- ◆ Our intention is to participate in the evolution of love.

   [*In the next few pages we will cover some key concepts which are essential to locating ourselves and setting the context for all the One Mountain, Many Paths Oral Essays. —Eds.*]

OVERVIEW: EROS IS NO LONGER A LUXURY—IT'S LOVE OR DIE

Eros is life.

The failure of Eros destroys life.

Our lack of Eros is poised to destroy the world.

All civilizations have fallen because the stories that they lived in were, in some sense, stories based on rivalrous conflict governed by win/lose metrics. Every civilization was weakened by interior polarization caused by the lack of a shared Story of Value.

We now have a global civilization, but we haven't created a shared Story of Value.

We haven't solved the generator functions that caused all civilizations to fall. Our global civilization has exponential technologies and extraction models depleting the Earth of resources that took billions of years to create, which is going to lead to a civilizational collapse.

Existential risk is risk to our very existence.

The choice is clear: love or die.

It's that simple.

Eros is no longer a luxury. It is an absolute necessity for the survival of the individual and the planet.

In the last half a century, modern psychology has documented an age-old truth: a fully nourished baby who is not held in loving arms will die.

So too, our world, both personal and global—even with all the resources of intelligence and technology at our disposal—will die without being held in love, in the embrace of Eros.

We must embrace a personal path of love and a global politics of love.

Not ordinary love. Not love which is "mere human sentiment," but Eros, or what we sometimes call Outrageous Love, which is the heart of existence itself.

We live in a world of outrageous pain.

The only response is Outrageous Love.

WHAT IS EROS?

Eros is the experience of radical aliveness, moving towards, seeking, desiring ever deeper contact and ever greater wholeness.[4] Eros is the core fabric of Reality's being and the motivational architecture of Reality's becoming.

Eros is what animates the evolutionary impulse itself, from the very inception of Cosmos all the way to our very selves, who awaken to the realization that the evolutionary impulse throbs uniquely in each of us.

The realization of human awakening and transformation that lies at the core of the interior sciences is the invitation—or even the urgent and desperate demand—of a madly loving Cosmos animated by infinities of power and infinities of intimacy.

The demand—the desperate invitation, the plea, the tender and fierce command of Cosmos that lives inside every human being—is to awaken: to awaken to our true nature as unique incarnations of Eros and Ethos that are needed and desperately desired by All-That-Is. Said slightly differently: Reality is Eros. Or: God is Eros.

The failure of Eros destroys life. The collapse of Eros is always the hidden (or not so hidden) root cause for the collapse of ethics.

This is true both personally and collectively. We live in a moment of a worldwide and personal collapse of Eros. Our lack of Eros is poised to destroy

---

4 We define Eros through what we refer to as the Eros equation (one of a series of what we call interior science equations):

Eros = Radical Aliveness x Desiring (Growing + Seeking) x Deeper Contact x Greater Wholeness x Self Actualization/Self Transcendence (Creation [Destruction])

There are good reasons for the formal language of the interior science equations in these writings, and the reader is invited to explore them on their own, in particular, in our work, David J. Temple, *First Principles and First Values: Forty-Two Propositions on CosmoErotic Humanism, the Meta-Crisis, and the World to Come* (World Philosophy and Religion, 2024).

the world. Humanity is currently experiencing what has come to be known as existential risk, a risk to our very existence, or what I will refer to as the Second Shock of Existence.

EXISTENTIAL RISK: THE SECOND SHOCK OF EXISTENCE

The first shock of existence is the death of the human being—the realization that we will die, which dawns in human consciousness at the beginning of history. We are not talking about the biological fact of death but the *existential* realization of death. Although the interior sciences disclose that death is a portal between two days (there is vast empirical,[5] philosophical,[6] and anthro-ontological evidence[7] for the continuity of consciousness[8]), death is also, in our own direct surface experience, a stark end. And that is obviously not a bug but a feature in the system.

---

5   We refer to evidence gathered by the most serious of researchers, beginning with Henry and Edith Sedgwick at Cambridge University and William James at Harvard University, and continuing in highly rigorous form for the last 150 years, as recapitulated by Whiteheadian scholar David Ray Griffin in multiple volumes. See also, for example, Dean Radin, *Real Magic: Unlocking Your Natural Psychic Abilities to Create Everyday Miracles* (Potter/TenSpeed/Harmony, 2018), *The Conscious Universe: The Scientific Truth of Psychic Phenomena* (HarperCollins, 2010), and other books. Or see the earlier classic by Frederic William Henry Myers, *Human Personality and Its Survival of Bodily Death* (Longmans, Green, 1907).

6   This requires a cogent analysis of materialism and dualism, and the introduction of the far more cogent third possibility which we have called "pan-interiority."

7   We discuss Anthro-Ontology in some depth in *First Principles and First Values*, and see also the fuller conversation in David J. Temple, *First Principles and First Values: Towards an Evolving Perennialism: Introducing the Anthro-Ontological Method*—both published by World Philosophy and Religion Press, in Conjunction with Integral Publishers. For now, we will simply define it as an "innate and clear interior gnosis directly available to the human being."

8   See Dr. Marc Gafni and Dr. Zachary Stein's essay in preparation, "Beyond Death: Anthro-Ontology, Philosophy, and Empiricism." This essay is slated to appear in the book *Towards a World Religion: Homo Amor Essays*. The essay is also the ground for a larger book by the same authors, *Twelve Portals to Life Beyond Death: Responding to the Second Shock of Existence*, in which we discuss three forms of material: the empirical, the philosophical, and the anthro-ontological, and show how each form discredits the notion of death as the end.

Our first-person experience is that death ends this life. It is not the *totality* of our experience if we go deeper inside, but it is obviously intended to be the central, potent, and painful dimension of every human life. Indeed, as Ernest Becker potently reminded us, the denial of death is at our peril.

All the stories and all the plotlines and all the threads of living end at that moment. Whatever happens beyond, we have an actual experience of ending. **Paradoxically, that ending, the experience of the finality of mortality, is what presses us into life.** From the implicit demand of the first shock of existence, human beings were activated and pressed into creative emergence, and what emerged was all of human culture, both interior and exterior.

The second shock of existence is the realization of the potential death of all humanity. After all the stages of human history—matter, life, and mind in all of their stages of evolutionary unfolding—we have come to this place in the evolution of humanity, in which the gap between our exponentially expanding exterior technologies and our stalled (or even regressing) interior technologies of value has created dire catastrophic and existential risks.

This gap generates extraction models and exponential growth curves, rivalrous conflicts based on win/lose metrics, tragedies of the commons, and multipolar traps, in which everyone has to keep producing to the nth degree, including weaponized exponential threats to our very existence because we are afraid that the other parties are going to do it and not be transparent—hide it from us and then dominate us.

GENERATOR FUNCTIONS FOR EXISTENTIAL RISK

Let's outline clearly the main *generator functions for existential risk.*

Rivalrous conflicts governed by zero-sum, win/lose metrics. Rivalrous conflicts generate extraction models at the core of the economic system and exponential growth curves. Both of these drive and are driven by a contrived system of artificially manufactured desires and needs, delivered into culture by ever more precise forms of micro-targeting to individuals and groups through the ever more immersive environment of the internet.

Next, rivalrous conflicts and exponential growth curves animated by win/lose metrics generate **complicated, fragile world systems** highly vulnerable to myriad forms of collapse. Fragile local systems are made exponentially more fragile on a global level by our inability to meet global challenges with social, legal, political, economic, and ethical infrastructures that remain largely local.

All of this is a direct result of the failure to develop more adequate interior technologies that would be sufficiently compelling to displace "rivalrous conflict governed by win/lose metrics" as the motivational architecture for the human life world.

This failure has led to the conditions that will cause the implosion of systems that are already and quite literally on the brink of collapsing themselves. That's what we mean by the *second shock of existence*.

To recapitulate: the second shock of existence is not the death of the human being, but the potential death of humanity.

It is the *Death Star* moment of our species.

THE DECONSTRUCTION OF INTRINSIC VALUE

We stand in this moment poised between utopia and dystopia, at a time between worlds and a time between stories. We need a new Story of Value, eternal yet evolving, rooted in First Principles and First Values, which would become a universal grammar of value and a context for our diversity.

This is exactly what the Renaissance was. It was a time between worlds and a time between stories. In the Renaissance, we had been recently challenged by the Black Death, a pandemic that swept across Europe. The Black Death destroyed between a third to half of Europe and a huge part of

Asia. People died horrifically, brutally, in the streets. They had no idea how to meet this challenge, and so, in response to the Black Death, da Vinci and Ficino and their cohorts understood that they had to tell a new Story of Value.

That story was the story of modernity. Did they get it right?

- They got part of it right, which birthed, to use Jürgen Habermas' phrase, "the dignities of modernity," such as new ways of gathering information and universal human rights.
- But they also deconstructed the source of Value. They lost the basis for the Good, the True, and the Beautiful.

The basis used to be divine revelation: *God told us.* But this claim was owned by religion, and every religion began to overreach and over-claim. The revelation was thus often mediated through cultural categories and wasn't fully accurate.

> *Modernity threw out revelation, but was unable to establish a new basis for value.*

Value was just assumed to be real. As it says in the founding document of the American Revolution: *We hold these truths to be self-evident*—that is, *we don't really have a basis for value; we just take it as a given.*

In other words, modernity took out a loan of social capital from the traditional world. The source of value was never worked out.

And then, gradually, value began to collapse.

- The Universe Story began to collapse.
- The belief that the Good, the True, and the Beautiful are real began to collapse.
- The belief that Love is real began to collapse.

As Bertrand Russell is reported to have said, "I cannot see how to refute the arguments for the subjectivity of ethical values, but I find myself incapable of believing that all that is wrong with wanton cruelty is that I do not like it."

What do you do if you grew up in a world in which value is not real? A world without a source of value, without a Universe Story, without a story of human identity, without a story of desire, without a narrative of power?

In the words of W.B. Yeats, *the center does not hold.*

- You have a collapse at the very center of society, because you no longer have Eros.
- You no longer have a Reality in which value is real, and so you have this lingering sense of emptiness.
- You have a complete collapse at the very center.
- We become *the hollow men and the stuffed men*, gesture without form.

And that's the source of our current existential risk.

THE DEEPER ROOT CAUSE OF THE META-CRISIS: A GLOBAL INTIMACY DISORDER

Above, I have outlined the major generator functions of existential risk. But there is a deeper cause for the existential risk that lurks underneath the rivalrous conflict governed by win/lose metrics and the fragile systems they engender.

And we cannot take the Death Star down without discerning and addressing this. We have already alluded to this root cause above, but at this point we need to make it more explicit so that, from this context, the adequate root response will become clear.

Modernity threw out revelation, but was unable to establish a new basis for value.

This ostensibly surprising statement can be understood in a few simple steps:

1. All of the catastrophic and existential risk challenges we face are global: from climate change to artificial intelligence, pandemics, systems collapse, and exponential arms races.
2. Every global challenge self-evidently requires a global solution.
3. Global solutions can only be implemented with global co-ordination.
4. Global co-ordination is impossible without global coherence.
5. Global coherence is only possible if there is a global resonance between the parts.
6. Global resonance is only possible if we have global intimacy.

ONLY A SHARED STORY OF VALUE CAN GENERATE GLOBAL INTIMACY

Global intimacy—just like intimacy in a couple—is only possible when there is a shared story.

Not just a shared history, but a shared Story of Value.

- It is only a shared global story that can generate a new emergent quality of intimacy: global intimacy.
- A shared Story of Value must be rooted in shared ordinating values, or what we have called evolving First Values and First Principles.
- Intimacy requires a shared grammar of value as a matrix for a shared Story of Value.

The global intimacy disorder is the root cause for existential risk. The global intimacy disorder underlies the core generator functions for existential risk.

The global intimacy disorder is rooted in the failure to experience ourselves in a field of shared intrinsic value. This failure derives from the deconstruction of value.

Indeed, it is wholly accurate to say that **the root cause of the two generator functions of existential risk is the failed story of intrinsic value, or what we might also call the breakdown of Eros.**

1. The first generator function is **the success story**. Our modern success story is rivalrous conflict governed by win/lose metrics, which violates all the terms of the Intimacy Equation: there is no shared identity and no mutuality of recognition, feeling, value or purpose, and instead of *relative* otherness, there is *alienated* otherness. Such a story generates complicated fragile systems with no allurement or intimacy between the parts, systems which optimize for efficiency (as an expression of win/lose metrics) and not for resiliency and life.

2. The second generator function is **the deconstruction of intrinsic value** itself. The deconstruction of value is the sense that human value does not participate in the intrinsic value of the Real, for the Real is dogmatically declared to have no intrinsic value. Thus, there is no shared identity between the interior of the human being and Reality. There is no common participation in a field of shared intrinsic value. Instead of being intimate with value, we are alienated from value. And only intrinsic value can arouse will: political, moral, and social will.

To sum up, without a shared grammar of value there is no global intimacy, and therefore no global coherence, and no global coordination in response to catastrophic and existential risk, which means, put simply, there will be, quite literally, no future.

HEALING THE GLOBAL INTIMACY DISORDER REQUIRES THE EVOLUTION OF INTIMACY

But we are not hopeless. On the contrary, we are filled with great hope. Hope is a memory of the future. That memory of the future *is* the direct hit that takes down the Death Star, the culture of death. **The direct hit must be**—as it has always been in history—**the emergence of a new stage of evolution**.

Crisis is an evolutionary driver, and every crisis is, at its core, a crisis of intimacy: from the oxygen crisis of the single cells dying which generated multicellular life at the dawn of existence, to the existential risk in this very moment.[9]

The direct hit is therefore structurally self-evident: the evolution of intimacy itself.

What is intimacy, as a structure of Cosmos all the way down and all the way up the evolutionary chain? We engage this inquiry in depth in other writings, but for now we will simply adduce what we have called the "Intimacy Equation":

Intimacy = shared identity in the context of [relative] otherness x mutuality of recognition x mutuality of pathos x mutuality of value x mutuality of purpose

Intimacy is about the capacity of parts to generate a *shared identity* while retaining their otherness, or distinct identity. This requires multiple mutualities, including recognition, pathos (or feeling), value, and purpose. The parts must recognize and feel each other, even as they share value and purpose. But all of this must lead to intimate union—and not pathological

---

9 We demonstrate this principle in some depth in the multi-volume series, *The Universe: A Love Story* (forthcoming) (https://worldphilosophyandreligion.org/early-ontologies), *The Intimate Universe: Global Intimacy Disorder as Cause for Global Action Paralysis* (forthcoming), and in other writings of CosmoErotic Humanism.

fusion, where the distinct identity of the parts disappears—like subatomic particles that successfully become an atom, or two people who successfully become a couple.

THE DECONSTRUCTION OF VALUE IS THE DECONSTRUCTION OF INTIMACY

We have identified the global intimacy disorder as the root cause of existential risk. But the underlying ultimate failure of intimacy is the deconstruction of value itself.

The deconstruction of value means that human value does not participate in any sense of intrinsic value of the Real. This is not about individual *values,* but about *the Field of Value* that underlies all of them. **When the human being**—moved, often sincerely or even nobly, by myriad cultural, historical, and psychological confusions—**claims to have stepped out of the Field of Value, then intimacy itself is deconstructed.**

The deconstruction of value is the deconstruction of intimacy.

In the absence of a shared Story of Value, a story that is an authentic expression of Reality's Eros, a story rooted in *pseudo-Eros* takes center stage and becomes the generator function for existential risk. Our modern pseudo-Eros story is *rivalrous conflict governed by win/lose metrics.* Such a story catalyzes in its wake the second generator function of existential risk: *complicated fragile systems with no allurement or intimacy between the parts.* It is in that sense that we have argued that the first generator function for existential risk is the success story.

- ◆ The failure of intimacy is precisely the impotent experience that there is no shared identity between the interior of the human being and Reality. **There is no shared identity in the sense of any kind of common participation in a field of shared intrinsic value.**
- ◆ **But only a shared Story of Value can arouse the global will**

required to engage catastrophic and existential risk. For it is only global political, moral, and social will—and we can even say *erotic* will—that can generate the most Good, True and Beautiful world that we have always known is possible.

THE EVOLUTION OF LOVE IS THE TELLING OF A NEW STORY

Coupled with the Intimacy Equation is the scientifically grounded realization, in both the exterior and interior sciences, that Reality is a progressive deepening of intimacies, or, said slightly differently:

Reality is Evolution. Evolution is the evolution of intimacy.

- The evolution of intimacy requires—both personally and collectively—a deeper, more accurate discernment of the nature of our universe, ourselves, and our beloveds.
- This new discernment generates a new global Story of Value.
- The new global Story of Value generates an emergent, heretofore unseen global intimacy and heals the global intimacy disorder.

The new Story of Value is the direct hit that takes down the Death Star and replaces it with the hope that invokes the memory of our best future.

Global intimacy facilitates global coherence, which facilitates global coordination, which activates the possibility of our creative and effectively coordinated global responses to the global meta-crisis in its entirety and its specific expressions.

To solve Bertrand Russell's challenge—the apparent argument for the subjectivity of ethical values—**we have to reground value theory in eternal yet evolving First Principles and First Values, and articulate a new Story of Value.**

This is what we call CosmoErotic Humanism.

CosmoErotic Humanism—together with other emergent strands—**needs to become the ground of a world religion as a context for our diversity**. We need religion, even as we need science, to articulate a shared global grammar of value.

As we said at the beginning, our choice is simple: love or die.

- To love means to participate in the evolution of love, which is the evolution of the human Story of Value.
- To love means to evolve and activate a new cultural enlightenment—rooted in a new narrative of identity, a new narrative of value, a new narrative of intimate communion, a new narrative of desire, a new narrative of power—all of which will birth new narratives of economics and politics.
- The evolution of love is the telling of a new story.

The new story that must be told is a love story, for in fact that is the deepest truth of Reality, rooted in the best exterior and interior sciences, that we have at this moment in time:

- Reality is not merely a fact. Reality is a story.
- Reality is not an ordinary story. Reality is a love story.
- Reality is not an ordinary love story. Reality is an Outrageous Love Story.

Story doesn't mean it's *made-up*.

It means doing the hard work of integrating the validated insights of the traditional world, the modern world, and the postmodern world.

This is the intention at the heart of telling the new story of CosmoErotic Humanism.

ABOUT THIS VOLUME

The world today faces a "meta-crisis"—a series of unprecedented, inter-locking challenges that threaten both our individual and collective survival. The meta-crisis highlights the urgency for a profound transformation, not just of all our exterior systems, but of our interiors, of the very Story of Value, that is the inescapable framework that shapes all dimensions of our reality. *Homo Amor and Unique Self* explores several fundamental dimensions of this new Story of Value.

It is only a new Story of Value that will overcome what Gafni has identified as the root cause of the meta crisis: the global intimacy disorder. All intimacy disorders, personal or global, are rooted in the prior collapse of a shared Story of Value. Therefore, the overcoming of the disorder and the emergence of a new intimacy can only be rooted in a new shared Story of Value, CosmoErotic Humanism.

Homo amor is the answer to the one of the three great questions of CosmoErotic Humanism, Who Am I, or Who are We? The evolution of consciousness which itself is the evolution of love is rooted in the *ever deepening* response to this great question of human identity. Indeed, *Homo amor* is the next evolutionary step beyond *Homo sapiens*, because *Homo amor* is a deeper, truer, and more beautiful answer to the question of our identity. *Homo amor* is the new human and new humanity. *Homo amor* is the CosmoErotic Universe in person. The new human has a direct realization that the Eros, allurement, and intimate yearning of her life are interwoven into the unfolding fabric of Cosmos itself. In other words, not only is the personal the political, but the personal is the cosmic.

This is the shift in identity that changes everything. When you realize that you are the personal face of the pulsing evolutionary heart of Amorous Cosmos, you engender a radical transformation in every dimension of your personal life—and in reality itself. This is what Dr. Marc Gafni and Barbara Marx Hubbard call a "Planetary Awakening in Love through Unique Self Symphonies."

At the heart of this awakening is a deeper answer to the question of Who Are You than has ever been available in culture. This is the realization we are each a Unique Self. To be a Unique Self is to know yourself directly as the irreducibly unique expression of the Eros and energy of all that is, that lives in you, as you, and through you, and that never was or will be ever again other than through you. Unique Self rejects the prevalent flatland view of modernity in which the self is understood to be but a skin-encapsulated ego.

The individual as an isolated entity caught in never-ending rivalrous dynamics governed by win/lose metrics generates the fragile systems that lead to existential risk. In direct contrast, Unique Self is understood to be your irreducibly unique expression of the Eros Value that animates the entire Cosmos. Unique Self is an embodied gnosis that recognizes each person as a unique configuration of Eros, intimacy, desire, and consciousness, as well as a unique set of allurements, whose unique gifts and unique quality of Eros and intimacy is intended, recognized, chosen, adored, desired, and needed by All-That-Is.

Volume 22

These oral essays are edited talks delivered by Marc Gafni between September 2019 and February 2024.

CHAPTER ONE

THE PUZZLE PIECE DHARMA
AND THE FIVE SELVES

Episode 155 — September 28, 2019

A COLLECTIVE HUMAN INTELLIGENCE IN UNIQUE SELF SYMPHONY IS THE ONLY FORCE MORE INTELLIGENT THAN ARTIFICIAL INTELLIGENCE

I just want to set very gently our intention in Church. What are we here to do? Our Code is going to be about the Unique Self Symphony. It's about *can we come together as a world and create a Planetary Awakening in Love through Unique Self Symphonies.*

But what we're describing is not a few enlightened people, not an elite that's leading the way. **We're describing a groundswell uprising of Evolutionary Love. It's a grassroots uprising. It's a populist uprising, in which we feel Evolutionary Love driving the self-organizing universe, like it always has—but this time, it becomes conscious.** It begins to live in us in a way that we each choose to commit our Outrageous Acts of Love.

We choose to join the Unique Self Symphony, and we choose to play our instruments. We need that unleashing of an exponential force of a new configuration of intimacy, a new configuration of human beings, all over the world.

In an ant colony, ants all know what to do, and they do it on automatic pilot; but that automatic pilot is driven by the secretion of pheromones. Each ant knows what to do, and the ant colony operates. But we need not an ant colony—we need a Unique Self Symphony. Because human beings aren't ants. Human beings can actually choose dystopia or utopia.

So what's going to drive us to this Unique Self Symphony? What's going to get us home? What's going to create a world in which everyone's doing exactly what they need to do to give their unique gift, to unleash this exponential power of love and transformation?

What drives this Unique Self Symphony is: *everyone is driven—invited, moved by, allured by—their Unique Self.* **It's your Unique Self that tells you what you need to do.**

We're confronted by the threat of artificial intelligence outstripping human intelligence, and there's only one gorgeous force that stands against that, an intelligence that outstrips artificial intelligence completely. You know what that is? Unique Self Symphony.

Humans have the capacity to self-organize and create a collective human intelligence that outstrips anything you can possibly imagine.

Our intention is to come together in Evolutionary Love, to love each other so madly, so deeply, so beautifully, as consciousness awakening in us, that the world becomes an explosion of *Amor. Amor: its insides are lined with love.* We're here to lay down the structures, the *dharma*, and the memes that will allow the score of that Unique Self jazz Symphony to explode its gorgeous music all over the world.

As we set the intention, I wanted just to also find it in the world of song and the world of chant.

Let's add one piece so we can just feel what it's like to be together. There's these two lines that came down about four months ago, and they capture the words that David wrote in Psalms. I'll give you the original Hebrew, and then we'll get these two lines that capture the feeling of Unique Self Symphony. Then we'll turn to David who will resonate our code, and we'll feel it through him. Then we'll enter into prayer.

So here's a chant, so we can feel it on the inside. Pythagoras said that *music is the language of the Cosmos*. It's the mathematics of intimacy of the Cosmos. That's why we chant—it's the key that opens up the door.

In order to chant, you don't need to have a good voice. I'm the prime example of it, and I've been chanting for forty years.

You just need to rip your heart open, and let yourself stake your life on the fact that you can actually enter the inside of consciousness and feel it awake and alive.

Mizmor shir leyom ha'Shabbat	*It's good to sing a song of Thee.*
Tov lehodot L'Adonai	*It's good to chant as We.*
Lehagid baboker chasdecha	*To speak of your love in the morning*
Ve-emunatcha baleylot	*And trust you in the night.*

Evolutionary Church is where we come to live on the other side.

This is where the awakening has already happened.

This is where new humans gather.

This is where *Homo amor* is born.

We look at each other heart-to-heart—one love, one heart—and we open our inner eye, and we say to each other: *to speak of your love in the morning and to trust you in the night.*

EVOLUTIONARY LOVE CODE: THE FIELD OF INTIMACY AND DESIRE IS SEAMLESS BUT NOT FEATURELESS

The Field of Intimacy and Desire is seamless but not featureless.

The field is always moving to greater intimacy.

We are each unique features of the larger Field of Intimacy and Desire. That means we are each a unique configuration of desire and intimacy that is part of this larger field.

That field itself is generating a new structure of intimacy, which is the Unique Self Symphony.

WE GET TO FALL MADLY IN LOVE WITH EACH OTHER

The beginning of a Unique Self Symphony is the experience that we get to fall madly in love with each other. We actually realize: *Who am I? I am a unique configuration of intimacy and desire.* Desire is the desire to create a better future. Desire means *I want something. I want the next second to be so beautiful and so gorgeous. I want my heart to be open.*

We don't want to go beyond desire. We love desire. As the Buddha said, *Have few desires, but have great ones.*

A great desire is a clarified desire. A great desire is the desire you want to have on the day of your death.

- ◆ It's the desire that you're proud of.
- ◆ It's the desire that you can sign your name on.
- ◆ It's the desire for ever deeper contact and ever greater wholeness.

- It's the desire to love the moment open.
- It's the desire to give your unique gift.
- It's the desire to feel the radical aliveness of Reality moving through you, and to have the desire for every other human being to feel it as well.

From that place, we get to fall in love with each other.

We've exiled falling in love: "It's a human experience. It means infatuation. It's with one person. It's supposed to feel the same way your whole life, and when it doesn't, you're devastated and you feel like your life's a failure."

That's the beginning of the collapse of our culture.

In a Unique Self Symphony, we're each playing our instrument, and we're madly in love with each other's instrument. It's a jazz Symphony. So in different moments, each person comes forth and plays. And we get to fall in love with each other.

RECLAIMING A POLITICS OF LOVE

In this Evolutionary Church, we're reclaiming a politics of love.

- Politics is right here, right now.
- Politics is a good thing.
- Politics means life.
- Politics means living.

There's no split between politics and religion, although there might be a separation of church and state.

We've got to separate church and state, and bring politics and re-ligion back together.

But by religion, we don't mean *one religion*; we don't mean *somebody who owns the church*. We mean politics and God. Because how could you take God out of politics? We took God out of politics because one particular church—for example, the Catholic Church in Europe—hijacked God and said, "We own God." It used God as a form of abusive power-over.

So we said, let's separate these two things, let's separate church and state so we can't have that abuse. That was a great move. That was a momentous leap of modernity.

But now, in this meta-modern moment, in this new moment of *Homo amor* consciousness, we need to bring politics and religion back together—but we include all the religions. The one God, the one love, the one heart, that lives in me, as me, and through me, and holds me in the same moment. That's what politics is.

Politics is religion, and religion is politics.

It's about how we change this world, and how we speak to every single human being on the planet. We say: *Oh my God, you're gorgeous. You're beautiful. Oh my God, Mr. Tree, I want to fall madly in love with you. Oh my God, Mrs. Rock, you're awesome.*

Then we say that to each other, *We're here together. We're doing this together.*

GOD, CAN I BRING EVERYTHING TO YOU?

That's when we turn to God in prayer. We turn to Go,d and we say:

> *God—one love, one heart, who holds me, who knows me in every second—can I bring everything to you? Can I bring all of me to you? Can I bring my holy and broken Hallelujah to you?*

The word *Hallelujah* means *hallel*: pristine, gorgeous praise, the beauty of me, and *holelut*: drunken intoxication when I'm totally broken. **There's nothing more whole than a broken heart.**

So in the politics of God, in the religion of this world, it's all mixed up: politics and religion, they're one. And the Unique Self Symphony is an expression of a synergistic democracy—this is Barbara's word—where we come together and we self-organize, and we give our gifts. **But we can only give our gifts if we have a place to rest. We know that we're partnered with the Divine. We're held by God, and God is held by us; we hold hands and we jump together.**

But first, we've got to know that we're held and that we're never alone. Our broken *Hallelujah* and our holy *Hallelujah*—there's a blaze of light in every word, everything matters. Our lives are ultimately significant. We're all needed. So let's go to Leonard Cohen, and let's reclaim love as religion towards a politics of love.

Hallelujah, we ask for everything. We're reclaiming prayer. We turn to God not as the Infinity of Power, but as the Infinity of Intimacy. Evolution is the evolution of intimacy. The evolutionary impulse is one expression of the Divine. God desires deeper and more intimacy. The Infinity of Intimacy that knows our name.

We ask for everything because prayer affirms the dignity of personal need; we're significant, we matter. **We have to learn to pray because in prayer, we affirm the dignity of our own personal need.** This is not narcissism, which actually means, *I don't love myself.* Self-love means, *I'm a unique configuration of intimacy and desire, and my instrument is needed in the Symphony.*

We're going to lift these prayers to the sky, and we're going to lift them so high that we have the actual, lived experience of the evolutionary family.

PLANETARY AWAKENING IN LOVE THROUGH UNIQUE SELF SYMPHONY

We said at the beginning that our code is about a Planetary Awakening in Love through the Unique Self Symphony. The Unique Self Symphony is the next emergence of evolutionary intimacy, in which every human being realizes: *I'm an irreducibly unique expression of LoveIntelligence and Love-Beauty—I'm an irreducibly unique expression of the initiating energy and Eros of All-That-Is—that lives in me, as me, and through me, that hasn't been and never will be in anyone that ever was, is, or will be, other than through me.*

As such, I have a unique gift to give that stands on the abyss of darkness and says *let there be light*, and speaks to a corner of the world that's unloved.

So we're all politicians, and we're all priests, and we're all rabbis, and we're all imams, and we're all secular humanists. It's all of us. It's a democratization of greatness. It's a democratization of politics. But *I don't do it alone—I step into the Unique Self Symphony.*

The Field of Intimacy and Desire is seamless but not featureless. The field is always moving towards greater intimacy. **We are each unique features of the larger Field of Intimacy and Desire. That means we are each a unique configuration of desire and intimacy that is part of this larger field.**

That field itself is generating a new structure of intimacy, which is the Unique Self Symphony.

AUTHENTIC INTELLIGENCE: A CONSCIOUS INTENTION BY EACH OF US TO GIVE OUR UNIQUE GIFT

We talked about an anthill before. Imagine the image of a swarm intelligence. At the leading edges of science, we now know that a key way to potentiate wisdom—a brilliance and a gorgeousness beyond anything that artificial intelligence can generate—is to move from artificial intelligence to authentic intelligence.

Authentic intelligence means that we gather human beings around the planet and we create a kind of swarm intelligence—but the swarm intelligence is not unconscious, as it is in an anthill or a beehive. Rather, **it's a conscious decision by each of us to give our unique gift, guided by the impulse of our uniqueness and the allurement of our uniqueness; the unique configuration of intimacy and desire that wants to move together and move beyond egoic win/lose metrics, and come together as the synergistic Unique Self Symphony.** The move to overcome the threat of artificial intelligence is the move from artificial intelligence to authentic intelligence. And authentic intelligence is the intelligence of Evolutionary Love.

Then we begin to actually create a Unique Self Symphony. Then we can say: *Hey, brother. Hey, sister. There's nothing in this world that I wouldn't do for you. Because you're my brother, you're my sister, and I can feel you. Because you're part of this Unique Self Symphony.*

Let's feel it. Our brother Avicii, who sang this song, sadly got so seduced and manipulated and moved by win/lose metrics that he committed suicide. He couldn't feel the Unique Self Symphony that he was trying to create, because it got monetized and commodified.

So we're going to build this Church, but it's never going to get monetized and commodified. This is our Church, this is One Church, where we are reclaiming love as religion. Love is in the details, and it's Outrageous Love. It's *all the way*, and *nothing is left out*.

THE DHARMA OF THE FIVE SELVES

There are five selves.

1. The first self is separate self. Separate self is real: *I embrace my story, the dignity of who I am, and I take responsibility.*

It's gorgeous, but it's limited because I'm not just a separate self. A separate self is ultimately incapable of creating a Unique Self Symphony. Unique Self Symphony is an evolutionary "we-space," while separate self is ultimately separate. *I'm a puzzle piece, but there's no puzzle*; we can't get it together. That's why Heidegger said, *people never actually get over their loneliness* because we're separate selves, and you can never traverse that chasm that separates you from others. So the only thing left is the rivalrous success story, based on win/lose metrics: *it's me against you*. Separate self cannot create a Unique Self Symphony.

2. Then there's the false self, which the shadow split-off. *I can't look at the real issues.*

False self means I'm living in a false self sense. My false core belief is: "I'm not enough. I'm not special. I'm always going to be alone." Or: "I'm too much, the world can't take me." Or: "I'm broken, I'm bad." That's my false self, this essential brokenness in me. That brokenness is really my false core, and I build a false self to cover it up. A false self can't create evolutionary we-space because it's not just a puzzle piece that's separate, but the puzzle piece is crumpled up; you can't even put it together in any way. **There's no sense of a bigger puzzle; you've just got a bunch of crumpled up puzzle pieces that can't fit together, and it doesn't work**.

3. Then there's True Self. That's the dramatic jump into enlightenment. It's the beginning, it's the first step: I realize that *I'm part of the seamless coat of the Universe.*

But the seamless coat of the Universe, the one love, one heart, is seamless but not featureless, and its features are consciousness all the way across: one love, one heart, one consciousness. The total number of True Selves in the world is one. See, here's the problem. When I become part of the One True Self—one love, one heart, one consciousness—I also can't create an evolutionary we-space because "we" always has two. It's two that become one, but it's still two.

So in True Self, we say, "**there's only a puzzle, and those lines that separate between the different parts of the puzzle piece are just an illusion.** Meditate, and the delusion will go away. Distinction, individuality, and individuation are all actually illusions."

10

We move beyond separation, but *there's only one.* So you can't create a Unique Self Symphony, because symphony comes from diversity, from something which has two that are in union. So True Self, the classical teaching in enlightenment, cannot create a Unique Self Symphony.

4. Then there's Unique Self. I realize the Universe is seamless, not featureless.

The feature is not only consciousness—it's my unique configuration of consciousness. It's not just consciousness—it's allurement, intimacy, and desire.

- ◆ I'm a unique configuration of intimacy and desire.
- ◆ I'm a unique configuration of Evolutionary Love.
- ◆ I'm a puzzle piece, my puzzle piece fits perfectly into the puzzle.
- ◆ I'm held by being fit into the puzzle.
- ◆ I complete the puzzle in some particular way.

But even Unique Self can't quite get you there. Unique Self is the beginning, but even Unique Self can't quite create a Unique Self Symphony; it can't quite create an evolutionary we-space. We need to go to the final stage.

5. Evolutionary Unique Self, *Homo amor.*

Evolutionary Unique Self is Unique Self in an evolutionary context, where we realize that *we are all beating with the evolutionary impulse.*

- ◆ The evolutionary impulse and Eros moves through all of us, and we're part of the same movement towards evolutionary intimacy.
- ◆ Evolution is awakening in us and depends on us coming together.
- ◆ We're living in this larger evolutionary context.
- ◆ We have a shared evolutionary relationship to life.

As Evolutionary Unique Selves, as Homo amor, we come together and create an evolutionary we-space.

Not only does our puzzle piece complete the puzzle, not only are we held by the puzzle, but we're also *evolving* the whole puzzle. My puzzle piece is necessary to evolve the whole puzzle.

Our music comes together.

PLANTING THE DHARMA IN POLITICS, SCIENCE, RELIGION, JUSTICE, GOVERNMENT, AND RELATIONSHIPS

I want to point out something truly exciting about being the evolution of intimacy and desire ourselves. We have been talking about humanity at the shift point between devolution, terrible destruction, and pain on one side, and the evolution of love, creativity, and potentiality on the other side of the shift. So this morning as I was reading this Code, I declared, *I'm on the other side of the shift, and I'd like you all to come with me*—because our unique desire is God's desire for intimacy.

I want to take a moment in this sermon to declare, reveal, and discover how it's happening in every cultural aspect of our lives. It's very hard to see because it's not the news. The news is everything that *isn't* working. **The new news is everything that's emerging.** Here's what I saw, and then we'll see how we can place it into the church. The church itself, as it was in the early church, is the place where we gather for the entire *dharma* to come through. But I was just reflecting on how that *dharma* has come through me.

I decided, for example, to bring *dharma* into politics. So without any possibility of being Vice President of the United States, I [Barbara] decided to

12

run to be selected as the Vice President so I could make a speech for us all, to say that the new politics is activating, connecting, and expressing what's working and new and emerging in the world. Okay, so we planted it there.

Then, let's take science. As were writing *The Universe: A Love Story*, we took all the latest scientific and psychological truths and wove them into the formation of the love story of this new humanity. Let's bring science in there. My friends from the Intergalactic University show that the reality of contact with life beyond this planet has already been demonstrated hundreds if not thousands of times, but is not yet recognized by science. So we're saying that science is going to have to expand itself to include itself in this very reality.

Then let's take spirituality itself. What we're doing here is evolving spirituality very much in the way Jesus did. When he said: "If you've seen me, you've seen Reality. If you see me, I am you, and you are me." We are saying—along with Jesus, the Buddha, and every great religious leader—that we are that.

We are showing up in science. We are showing up in politics. We're showing up in religion. We're showing up in the media. We are now planting the seed of this emerging Reality in every discipline of society.

In the Evolutionary Church, I would like to invite us to see ourselves as post-shift, creating a place where everyone who is also shifting knows they can go to. We're not shifting into a vacuum. We're not shifting into a space with nobody in it. We're shifting into a space where all the new humans are congregating. We're shifting into a space where the desire of God for greater intimacy and Eros is happening through our joining. **If you're going to do the new science, the new politics, and the new spirituality, you have to join intimately with each other, where you overcome the illusion of separateness that keeps all these divisions separate from each other, including all the religions in the world.** We're overcoming all those divisions by the desire in each of us for intimacy with the Divine, with each other, and with the clusters of people now populating the social scene with the new humanity.

I believe that in the same short period that we could descend into devolution and destruction, we can also create new fields in every area of culture that we can see in that Wheel of Co-Creation, including justice, science, government, and relationships. All of them are being populated by exactly this desire and this intimacy, as well as this inner knowing that the book of life will not be written without each other.

Let us have a collective prayer in this moment for the culture of humanity, knowing that the desire of God is for greater intimacy in every field, and that this intimacy is now being realized.

In the Evolutionary Church, I would like us to celebrate the evolution of culture itself, in all these fields, with all these people now taking their step into the future—as the desire of God for greater intimacy, connectivity, and love.

CHAPTER TWO

TAKE YOUR UNIQUE RISK: GIVING UP BEING RIGHT

Episode 156 — October 5, 2019

STEPPING UP AS THE COMMUNITY OF GOD SELVES

It's so good to be with everyone. This is the beginning of a crossing point. This is the first time that I know of in history that a group of human beings have come together with an awareness that "I am *Homo amor*," that we are the fulfillment of *Homo sapiens*. We're going to talk about:

- What does that mean to be that fulfillment?
- What does it mean to be the fulfillment of *Homo sapiens* as *Homo amor*?
- What does it mean to realize that at this moment, as we stand in this juncture, we have the ability to literally invoke the next level of evolution?

Evolution is not *out there*. Evolution is the manifest God living in us, as us, and through us.

We're used to thinking about God as one. But actually, God is community. There's oneness in community, and community in oneness.

- God is community.
- God is a community of molecules.
- God is a community of cells.
- God is a community of societies.

15

Then those molecules and those cells wake up. Imagine for a second that your cell woke up. Does your cell wake up and say, *I'm part of Kristina?* Or, *I'm part of David?* No, your cell is doing its thing. It's operating unconsciously, animated by the intelligence of Cosmos.

But we human beings—in the cellular organism of humanity, of *God* as community made manifest and made alive—have the capacity to awaken and realize: *I, Marc, am a cell in the larger organism, and I am needed and my presence is needed, and my gift is needed, and I can affect and impact the entire system. My unique configuration of intimacy and desire, committing my unique Outrageous Acts of Love, can actually tilt Reality—in its interior and its exterior—towards hope, goodness, truth, and beauty. I am the Unique Self Symphony playing uniquely through me. It's a jazz symphony. So when I step up to commit my Outrageous Acts of Love, the entire world steps back so I can play my trombone, so I can play my trumpet, so I can play my clarinet.*

This awareness has never been true before. We are the community of God Selves. We are stepping up in this moment.

PRAYER: PULSING DESIRE MERGED WITH QUIVERING TENDERNESS

We're about to go into prayer. We're here in the One Church, reclaiming love as religion towards a practical pragmatic politics of love. **One of our core understandings is that we can pray**. This is not a dogma, and it's not a New Age assertion, and it's not a human potential claim; it's the deepest truth of the interior sciences. When we pray, we're not turning to the cosmic vending machine in the sky and putting in a quarter and getting out a new car. We're doing something so much more gorgeous and so much more profound.

Here's the meditation. Imagine your most intimate moment with your most intimate beloved. It might have been a son or a daughter. It might have been a friend. It might have been a co-worker. It might have been a wife or a husband. It might be a moment with a former wife or husband, where you caught each other's eyes and deeply understood each other for a moment. It's an intimate moment where you're ultimately together.

Imagine that moment of intimacy—and now double it, triple it, quadruple it, and exponentialize it. **Now to that moment of intimacy** of quivering, beautiful, gorgeous tenderness—**add your experience of the most intense and beautiful awakened sensual desire.**

Now take that desire—take the rocking of that desire, take the pulsing of that desire—**and merge it together with the quivering tenderness of that close moment** we described before, and put that quivering tenderness together with that pulsing desire. **And now exponentialize it, times a billion. Then imagine what the inside of God feels like.**

God is the Infinity of Intimacy, and God is the infinity of desire. God is loving you, desiring you personally, in this very moment, caring about every infinite jot and tittle, every detail of your life, every flutter of your heart. The Infinity of Intimacy is holding you and wanting you to be the most gorgeous that you can be. **Because when you're the most gorgeous that you can be, you become He/She; you actually realize your divinity; you become God/Goddess.** God/Goddess becomes more whole, more alive, more delighted, more powerful, more potentiated, as you become you.

God/Goddess says: *Please let me be with you. Know that I am you, and know that I'm holding you at the same time. Fall into my arms. I'm your Beloved, and I'm infusing my energy into you.*

Have you ever exchanged notes or exchanged texts or exchanged glances or exchanged bodies with a beloved, and your body is actually infused with the energy of your beloved? That's what prayer is. Prayer is *zivug im ha'Shechina*. It's the erotic merger with the Divine, coupled with a turning to that God/Goddess who's the Infinity of Intimacy. **God is not only the Infinity of Power. God is the Infinity of Intimacy that knows my name, that's holding me, and it is infusing me with Her/His essence in this moment.**

17

- We come to God as lover.
- We come to God as subject to the King.
- We come to God as brother/sister.
- We come to God as friend.
- We come to God as our most intimate one

We bring everything before God/Goddess. We ask for everything because prayer affirms the dignity of our personal need. We bring everything; nothing's left out.

- We're utterly naked before God.
- We bring our holy and we bring our broken *Hallelujah*.
- We know with utter and radical certainty that we're not alone.
- We're being held, madly loved, madly desired, madly penetrated, in this very second, even as the fullness of our open heart penetrates Goddess Herself.

So right now, we turn to the holy and the broken *Hallelujah*. We feel it inside, and we open it up, every single one of us individually, and every single one of us together.

I can't take my Unique Risk unless I affirm the dignity of my personal need and ask for everything.

I turn to the Infinity of Intimacy that's literally watching Marc talking now—that's watching every one of you, the Infinity of Intimacy that speaks these words, that's holding me, that's holding you, that's holding us right now—who wants to know: *What do you need?* **We only know what we need when we ask and we clarify our desire.**

Prayer is the clarification of our desire.

So what are we asking for?

EVOLUTIONARY LOVE CODE: IN ORDER TO COMMIT MY OUTRAGEOUS ACT OF LOVE, I MUST TAKE MY UNIQUE RISK

The Field of Intimacy and Desire is seamless but not featureless. The field is always moving toward greater intimacy.

We are each unique features of the larger Field of Intimacy and Desire. That means we are each a unique configuration of intimacy and desire that is part of this larger field. The field itself is generating a new structure of intimacy which is the Unique Self Symphony.

To join the field and play your instrument in the Unique Self Symphony, you must be willing to take your Unique Risk.

Your Unique Risk is always something that you can easily, in the public realm, get away with not doing.

You access your Unique Risk through deep listening in the quiet, through prayer, or through asking a group of close friends who know you well, what it might be.

We're accountable in life for only one thing: did we take our Unique Risk that all of Reality needed us to take? You don't take your Unique Risk once; you take your Unique Risk every day.

Our Code is about the realization that *I am a unique instrument in the Unique Self Symphony*. Now those words are dripping with meaning. For the last fifteen years I've been talking about this notion that every human being has—not in a Myers-Briggs test way, but in an intrinsic, innate, and essential way—a unique contribution that's needed by All-That-Is. *When I make that contribution, I become part of the Unique Self Symphony*. The next structure of politics is the Unique Self Symphony. Barbara said, "Unique Self Symphony—that's the synergistic democracy." So, we synergize together.

We want to model for Reality: *What does it mean for every human being to take their Unique Risk?* Every human being says:

1. Who am I? *I'm an Evolutionary Lover. I'm a Unique Self. I'm a unique configuration of Outrageous Love.* That's step one.
2. Step two: *As such, I have a unique gift and a unique contribution to make, that no one who ever was, is, or will be can make, other than me.*
3. Step three: *That is my Outrageous Act of Love.*
4. Step four: *When I make, when I do, when I be, when I activate myself, I commit my Outrageous Act of Love.*
5. Step five: *But in order to commit that Outrageous Act of Love, I've got to do one thing. I've got to take my Unique Risk.*

MY UNIQUE RISK IS, I'VE GOT TO PUT ALL OF MYSELF ON THE LINE, AND I DON'T KNOW EXACTLY HOW IT'S GOING TO GO

I want to talk about that just for a second now, what does it mean to take that Unique Risk? I remember when I was a kid, we used to go to Funfair. It was Exit 101 in upstate New York, in the Catskill Mountains. Remember *Dirty Dancing*? That's Catskill Mountains territory. So there I am, I'm like nine years old, and we're at Funfair, and we're skating. It's a roller-skating rink. There are boys and girls, and the big move is that the boy has to cross over to ask the girl, *Will you skate with me?*

I wanted to skate with Debbie Weinbach, an Orthodox Jewish girl from Borough Park. So I skated over, put my hand out, and said: *Debbie, would you skate with me?* She looked at me, and in that moment, there was this hesitation—*would she or wouldn't she?*—and all of Reality stopped. Then she put her hand out, and we started skating. Wow!

It's now like a year later, and Debbie Weinbach hasn't come back to the bungalow colony. I lived in Columbus, Ohio, and she lived in Borough Park, so I couldn't skate with Debbie Weinbach. But my heart opens again, because we have to love again. So I'm going to skate with Felicia. This time, I skate over and say: *Felicia, will you skate with me?* She looked at me and burst into tears. Then she turned around and skated off the rink and doesn't appear the rest of the night because she was just so overwhelmed by the request. We never talked the rest of the summer, and not once since then. Wow!

You know what our Unique Risk is? *We've got to skate over. We've got to put our arm out.* Sometimes Debbie is going to say yes, and sometimes Felicia is going to burst out crying and say no. **That's what the Unique Risk is. It means I've got to put all of myself on the line, and when I put all of myself on the line, I don't know exactly how it's going to go.** But I'm willing to skate over. I'm willing to extend my hand, knowing full well that my hand might either be clasped and held, or it might not be, and she might burst out into tears.

THE UNIQUE RISK OF THE INFINITY OF INTIMACY

You know what it means for the Infinity of Intimacy to create a world? You know what it means for Infinity to manifest finitude in the finite? What is God doing? The essence of Reality is that God is saying: *I'm going to take my Unique Divine Risk. I am Infinity of Power. I am the president of all presidents. I'm in charge of everything. Yet, I've got to take a risk to love. I can't just love by myself in the infinite Cosmos. I have to manifest Reality. I have to extend my hand to the finitude that I've manifested, and say:*

- Will you take my hand?
- Will you skate with me?
- Will you love with me?
- Will you create with me?
- Will you cry with me?
- Will you laugh with me?

Imagine the feeling of Divinity when we say *No*. Imagine the feeling of Divinity when we say: *You know what, God, I'm not going to take my Unique Risk with you. I can't do it.* Imagine God's feeling when we're in our contraction, when we're in our egoic posturing. And egoic posturing takes on so many disguises.

NO ONE WILL CALL YOU OUT FOR NOT TAKING YOUR UNIQUE RISK

Here's the nature of the Unique Risk: no one's going to call you out on it. You can explain exactly the game theoretic dynamic of why you're doing it, and why you've got to take care of the larger whole, and make sure that your career is going well so you can serve the most amount of people. You work it all out.

People don't take their Unique Risks "for the best reasons." The best people are best at explaining the best of reasons for taking your Unique Risk. There's no one who's going to call you out on it for not doing it because no one knows what it is. It's known only to you in your deepest quiet. Or if you get together with two or three really honest friends away from the maddening crowd, and you ask them what your Unique Risk is, they'll know too.

But it's a place where you have to say: *Oh my God, this is where my integrity lives. This is the place where if I take that Unique Risk, if I put my hand out no matter what happens, this is the purpose of my life.* I take my Unique Risk at certain key pivoting junctures in my life when I say *Yes*, and I take it in every second. Sometimes it's very hard to do.

HOW TO TAKE YOUR UNIQUE RISK: YOU PUT EVERYTHING ON THE LINE

A couple of days ago, Kristina and I had a big morning fight. I can't remember what it was about; I never remember what it's about. I was pretty sure I was entirely right. So I've got to take my Unique Risk, we've got to come back together. I have to give up being right. That's a Unique Risk.

We've got to give up being right. So there I was, I called Kristina and I said, *I'm so sorry.*

---

*That's how you take your Unique Risk.
You put everything on the line.*

+ You give up being right.
+ You give up the contraction of ego.
+ You give up how it's going to look.
+ You give up, and you're willing to risk the pain of the utter *it's just not going to work.*

It doesn't matter if we're held accountable for anything in the world—although we are held accountable because we count. **We're held accountable because our lives matter infinitely.**

The actual realization of this moment in time, as we are between devolution and evolution, is that we can come together as the Unique Self Symphony, not just an individual. **We come together and we realize that by taking our Unique Risk and playing our unique instrument, we become part of the self-organizing universe.**

There's no longer a split between politics and religion. I've been talking about it in the ways that I have for the last decade and that's what Barbara believed in. There is no split between politics and religion. The One World Church is a political body, and a new political party is a religious body. We've got to get over that split.

Yes, there's a separation between church and state, but not between politics and religion. Not one specific religion; not Christian, or Jewish, or Buddhist, or Catholic. But religion means to *religare*: to connect with the whole thing. **It's to know that my Outrageous Act of Love—which I take as a function and expression of my Unique Risk—is a cell in the self-organizing universe, in the Unique Self Symphony, that can change the whole thing.** Imagine a cascading wave building torrentially throughout the world, as this Church of Evolutionary Love grows.

There have to be lots of big and little Evolutionary Churches all over the world, each one a Unique Self Symphony. Those Unique Self Symphonies are connected through the dots, and there's a self-organizing political wave of Evolutionary Love, of people committing Outrageous Acts of Love in their unique circles of intimacy and influence, and the world becomes a place we can live in.

Now we've created a tomorrow, and we've returned literally to the Garden of Eden, in a way that we never could have been in the Garden of Eden.

We can manifest what it means to be a human being, which is what it means to be God.

WE ARE GOD IN EVOLUTION AND WE ARE AT A SHIFT POINT OF EVOLUTION

Marc, my sermon is so inspired by who I am as I'm listening to you, that I am now going to go the whole way with who I am, because it deeply inspired me out of my ordinary position in life. I'm sure this is true for all of us. Following you doing a sermon requires a certain amazing presence of mind from your friend, Barbara, which is why I thought I would go the whole way.

So it starts out with the phrase: I am God in evolution. I'm going to take this literally, that we, you, all of us, are that entire force of creation. The genius that it took to go the 13.7 billion years to me and you now at the very crossroads of evolution, where the system could go into devolution, or rise into the next stage of evolution. This means that every single individual is on that shift point. It's a punctuated equilibrium because evolution is concerned more with purpose than with species.

The purpose of each of us now in this Evolutionary Church is: I am God in evolution. **I am an expression of the uniqueness of who I am as God in evolution.** Every one of us is offering an absolutely required contribution to the whole system, at the point of devolution or evolution.

So we're giving thanks for living at this exact moment of history, where each person as God in evolution can affect the direction of the whole system—because each of us is intrinsic to the intimacy of the system that we are part of. **Every cell in our body can affect the whole body, every cell in the planetary body can affect the planet.**

Now I'm considering every person in the Evolutionary Church as an expression of divine creativity, uniquely who we are, coming together like nature does into synergistic convergence, both on the inner plane of love and spirit and prayer, and on the outer plane of co-creative action. I'm beginning to see this Church of Evolutionary Love as an expression—the first on this Earth to arise that I'm aware of—of what is truly a cluster of humans who believe that:

- I am God in evolution.
- I am the intention of creation.
- I am the intimacy of desire of the greater process of evolution.

We are coming together in synergistic convergence and realization of our desires, through prayer, through co-creation, and through all the developments that the Church is bringing to us, in collaborative and other ways of us joining together.

That's how you take your Unique Risk.
You put everything on the line.

I really see that at every one of these shift points of evolution, when it could have gone into greater devolution, there was always a species somewhere that connected enough separate parts to take a jump—from single-celled to multi-celled to animal to human—and now we are at the jump point.

Through the joining of genius—through unique vocational arousal of each member of this Church, unique and brilliant as each of us is, and as more of us come in—we can imagine the effect that this congregation of evolutionary impulse, genius, desire, and intimacy could have on the evolutionary shift point that we're in now.

It's like the early church, when a few people got together and believed Jesus, and believed in the second coming of Christ, were willing to go into lion's dens, die for this, give their lives for this. If we are as great as that, believing in the second coming of humanity, believing in each of us as an expression of the impulse of creation, incarnate as you and me, joined in a cluster of shared purpose. **Nature doesn't care for species—nature preserves purpose.**

I'd like to conclude this thought with the enormous purpose of the Church of Evolutionary Love, as a critical expression at this shift point of evolution, when evolution can go in whatever direction we're going in. I mean, we're the ones making up evolution right now. That's what all of this means.

So I'd like to take a moment of us to imagine the entire Evolutionary Church, all over the world as it grows, being critical to the shift point of evolution.

Evolutionary Church can be the activator, the inspiration of us coming together as a whole species, capable of healing the Earth, freeing ourselves from hunger, disease, war, and suffering. Such that we can penetrate into a universe of billions of other galaxies, and planets, many of which are said have as comfortable conditions as our own.

This is the moment, and in this moment, I am now asking for our contribution to the Evolutionary Church, seeing this Evolutionary Church as instrumental in the shift point because of the memes we're carrying.

I believe that Marc's memes are the precise memes required for the cultivation of a culture of co-creation in this world. I believe they are the precise means. That means that for every one of us attracted to this particular memetic code, how much can we give now to make this Church seminal in the evolutionary shift point of our generation?

Not only does contribution make a difference locally, for you and your small group. It makes a big difference because it is embodying the code of the shift point of humanity, especially if we get enough people worldwide, and small churches everywhere. We are at the shift point of our culture when we put this funding into our Church. I know that there's no other activity I'm part of, no other place where each of our voices can be heard at this level, other than this Evolutionary Church.

Let its song go out to the entire throng of humanity with our contributions.

CHAPTER THREE

CLARIFYING YOUR HEART'S DESIRE

Episode 157 — October 12, 2019

WE CAN ALL BE PROPHETS OF THE NEW WORD, BUT WE MUST BE COMMITTED

When the word comes through clearly, we can actually feel a new prophecy emerging. But the prophets are all of us. **All of us are prophets when we participate together and when we dedicate our lives.** Just like we can all be physicists, we can all be prophets of the new word. Prophecy is not just for the elite. But, just like becoming a great physicist, you've got to dedicate your entire life. *I want to clarify the word as it moves in me.* It's not, *I'm running my business*, or *I'm doing this, I'm doing that.* No, it's full-on.

That's why I was so delighted to join genius with Barbara, with someone who, in her words, vibrates on the same frequency. We were just so delighted to spend all of our lives, every waking moment and every sleeping moment, trying to clarify the *dharma*. But I want to invite everyone to step in. Not because *you have your dharma just because you said it.* No, not true. But only if you're willing to step in full-on, read day and night, clarify your motives, own your shadow, make mistakes and get up again, and to pray day and night.

Every single person can participate in the new prophecy. But what prophecy means is that it's not just facial recognition software, or the algorithm of artificial intelligence

—there's a deeper algorithm of intimacy that is the heart core and heart desire of Cosmos, and which lives uniquely in me, as me, and through me.

I am a unique expression of the standing and propagating waves of Cosmos, which are configurations of intimacy. I am a vessel, a *Merkabah*, a chariot.

I am an incarnation that holds a unique spark of the God voice, and I'm committed to accessing that God voice.

It's not a casual church service. It's not a casual synagogue. It's not a quick Islamic moment. It's not a secular humanist moment. It's not spending a weekend in Esalen. I'm committed. **The commitment of my lifetime, which is the commitment of a human being, is to clarify the God voice that lives in me, and to access the unique spark of that God voice.** Then I will have a prophecy to speak that the entire world needs to have spoken.

Now, sometimes the prophecy is spoken as the Sermon on the Mount; it's spoken atop the mountain. Sometimes it's under the Bodhi tree. Sometimes the prophecy is spoken in the kitchen late at night, or between lovers in the bedroom at 4am. Sometimes it's spoken to our children in the car, as we're picking them up from the carpool. Sometimes it's spoken at a restaurant with a friend.

The prophecy has many places; there are many great speeches to have. One of the books I got most upset about was a book by William Safire called *Great Speeches in History*, which only featured speeches by famous people in public spaces. That's not how it works.

The word prophet is *navi* in Hebrew. Remember the Na'vi in James Cameron's *Avatar*? He's actually playing with the Hebrew. *Navi* comes from the word *niv*, which means "the speech": the voice that lives in you, the unique voice that is yearning to come through you, the unique voice yearning to be spoken by you. **It's that unique voice that Reality is waiting for.**

We wake up as evolution, realizing that evolution lives in us, as us, and through us—and we know in the next moment that our desire is evolution's desire.

We're asking one question:

> Are you willing to clarify the unique God spark that lives in you, as you, and through you, that all of evolution conspired and breathed for billions of years to manifest? Are you willing to clarify that unique configuration of intimacy and desire, which is the unique gorgeousness and tenderness of your heart, the unique audacity and wonder of your being, the radical amazement of God/Goddess seeing through your eyes?

That is the statement:

> *I am evolutionary desire.*
>
> *I am Evolutionary Love.*
>
> *I am a unique configuration of Evolutionary Love and desire.*
>
> *I have a word to speak. That word is important. That word matters, and my speaking my word matters.*

The question this week is: *Are you willing to be a prophet?* Yes! *Borey niv sfatayim*: God creates the unique voice. Once I access my unique voice, then I'm a prophet.

What we're going to talk about this week is literally the instruction manual for the new human. The new human is not some weird new species. The new human is the fulfilment of *Homo sapiens* as *Homo amor*.

Homo amor is the human being who speaks the unique God spark, heart, voice, that lives in them, as them, and through them.

Homo amor knows: *my word matters; Reality needs my word.*

30

There's not one prophet. In the old world, there was one prophet. But you can't be a prophet just by saying something. **You've got to be a prophet because you're radically committed.**

Imagine you want to be this bodybuilder but you don't train. Remember Mr. Atlas from the comic books, when some of us were growing up? Say you're Mr. Atlas—but you never trained. Impossible. It's the same thing with prophecy.

To be a prophet, you have to train.

WE ARE A TRAINING SCHOOL FOR PROPHETS

What are we? We are a training school for prophets. We want to speak prophecy together. **Prophecy is your unique voice clarified.** There's no way that Barbara can speak your prophecy, and no way that Marc can speak your prophecy, and no way that any of us can speak each other's prophecy. But we all have to clarify, and we all have to train.

- To train means we open our hearts again and again.
- To train means we never leave the table.
- To train means we integrate our shadow.
- To train means we integrate and take into ourselves the split-off parts of ourselves, and we make ourselves whole.

Oh my God, we're going to be a kingdom of prophets, and a holy nation. That's what the One Church is, we're a kingdom of prophets and a holy nation, and everyone who wants to cross-train with us is welcome. It's cross-training: we have to train in our minds, our *soma*, our body, our heart, our psychology, our shadow work, our physics, our chemistry, our molecular biology. We train in all the great traditions: the premodern, modern, and postmodern.

We are training. So what are we?

We're a boot camp for new prophets. We need new prophecy.

Isaiah, Ezekiel, Lao Tzu, Sun Tzu. What did Sun Tzu say? He said, *I come to speak dangerous words, and I ask only that you listen dangerously.* So are we willing to listen dangerously?

That's our intention for this week.

Our intention is to listen dangerously.

Our intention is to be evolution.

- ◆ I am evolution.
- ◆ I am a unique configuration of Evolutionary Love.
- ◆ I am the prophet of evolution.
- ◆ I am the prophet. My voice is good, and my voice is trustable; you can trust my voice.

You remember the chant? *To speak of your love in the morning, and to trust you in the night.* It's like that.

Our first conversation today has been about the realization that *I can be a prophet.* Remember Khalil Gibran, who wrote that beautiful book, *The Prophet*? That's what Khalil Gibran understood. He understood that prophecy needs to be democratized—but not as a casual encounter. There's no casual sex and there's no casual prophecy, and there's no casual love. It's never casual. It doesn't work that way.

- ◆ It's intentional.
- ◆ It's alive.
- ◆ It's with the full feeling tone, and gravitas, and radical joy, and responsibility of Cosmos moving in me.

That's what it means to be a prophet.

32

Each of us has that unique God/Goddess spark, which is the word. But we speak that word not only in public; we also speak that word in private. You're always speaking prophecy when you speak from your clarified God voice, and you can actually feel when you're speaking from that voice.

We're here today to access how we do that.

IN PRAYER, WE INVOKE—IN PROPHESY, GOD INVOKES

Now we're about to go into prayer. So what's the relationship between prayer and prophecy? Remember, prayer is not a cosmic vending machine where I put in a quarter and get out a shiny new horse, or a horse and buggy, or a car. Prayer is the realization that Reality is not only impersonal, but that Reality is ultimately personal. Beyond the impersonal forces of Cosmos, there's a deeper dimension which is infinitely personal.

It's not as most people taught spirituality: "First you've got the human personality that's personal, then you've got the impersonal forces of Cosmos, including love and consciousness and awareness." No! You've got the human personality, which is a fractal-like refraction of the higher personal. So level one: human personality, personal. Then you've got what we call the impersonal, but I'd rather call it the transpersonal impersonal. It's the forces of Evolutionary Love, the third person of God; the forces of physics—the strong and weak nuclear, electromagnetic, and gravitational—are operating everywhere in Cosmos, and the force of Eros animates all of them. That's the third person of God. That's the impersonal, or the transpersonal.

But then, and let's catch this important piece of *dharma*, there's the supra-personal. It's personal plus. It's beyond impersonal transpersonal. **The supra-personal is the Infinite Personhood of the whole Cosmos. It's all personal.**

There's a face of God which is not just the forces of physics, but inhering in that and in all those forces is an actual intelligence and consciousness of

Cosmos. It inheres in the fractal waves, and the standing and propagating waves of Cosmos, in the entire vibrational field of Cosmos. There's a personal animating intelligence in that field. **That personal animating intelligence is the second face of God; it's the Infinity of Intimacy.**

In prayer, we initiate and we invoke through our own yearning for intimacy—through our own desire to be the God voice, through our own desire to be fully realized, through our own desire to wake up out of the torpid slumber of our routines—beyond banality to our true rapture and greatness.

It comes from that yearning in us, that inconsolable longing to be more, to be our authentic selves, and to be a unique configuration of Self that is us.

We initiate and we invoke.

In prayer, the intimacy that lives in us yearns for the Infinity of Intimacy to hold us.

We come to prayer audaciously, as a child, and we say: *God, Goddess, hold me. Infinity of Intimacy, love me.* **In prayer we initiate and we invoke. In prophecy, when God speaks to us, we're receiving God; we're listening. God initiates, and God invokes, and we're receiving.** To be a prophet is to clarify your Unique Self, to get so clear that you can actually hear the voice of God.

How do you hear that voice of God? You get so quiet, so clarified, so still, that the dynamic explosion of the God voice merges and awakens from the stillness. But what I'm describing is not metaphor—this is the actual physics of Cosmos. I've experienced it in my life, time and time again. This is the inner physics of the great lineages.

This is how we do it. In prophecy, God initiates and God invokes, and we're so quiet that we're able to receive God loving us open; we're loved open, we're Fucked opened by the Divine.[1] It's fierce!

In prayer, we turn to God, and we say: *God, we're going to come before you open, naked, and vulnerable. We want to be held by you.* We say to God, give me everything—because prayer affirms the dignity of our personal need. We say to God, give me everything so I can give You everything.

When we turn to God with that raw vulnerability and that nakedness of heart, we're loving God open; we're fucking God open.

The actual sacred text says, *Hakadosh Baruch Hu Mit A-vheh La'asot Dirato Ba-tachtonim*: the God Force yearns and lusts for our naked open heart, wanting to be received by the Divine.

That's our true yearning. The Divine is all of it, all authenticity. So in this moment, we come before God and we bring before God our holy and our broken *Hallelujah*.

Nothing is left out when we pray.

Let's bind these prayers together, because everyone's prayer is our prayer. Let's bind these prayers together and lift them to the sky.

Are we ready to go all the way in this lifetime? Are we ready to love it open like we never have before?

---

1 Fuck, in all of its expressions, seeks to articulate a dimension of lived Eros, which is both prior to and beyond all language and culture. Fuck cannot be denied. It is a demand which, on the one hand, lives in us and, on the other hand, is sourced in forces much larger than us. Its potency is precisely in its impersonal quality. It is exactly the paradox of that impersonal quality awakening personally in us that is the heart of both Fuck's peril and power.

When we choose Fuck, then Fuck becomes conscious of itself in us. This is movement from unconscious Fuck to conscious Fuck; it is in that moment that Fuck awakens as the sacred. When we deny Fuck, then Fuck demands its pound of flesh, virtually always devolving into its more pathological forms. The sexual usage of fuck is the penultimate expression of the sense of Fuck which is about contact and connection. It is in this precise sense that the sexual models the erotic. Or said differently, the small-lettered "fuck" of the sexual models the erotic, capital-F Fuck of Reality.

EVOLUTIONARY LOVE CODE: WE'RE ACCOUNTABLE IN LIFE FOR THIS QUESTION: DID YOU TAKE YOUR UNIQUE RISK?

The Field of Intimacy and Desire is seamless but not featureless.

The field is always moving toward greater intimacy.

We are each unique features of the larger Field of Intimacy and Desire.

That means we are each a unique configuration of intimacy and desire that is part of this larger field.

The field itself is generating a new structure of intimacy which is the Unique Self Symphony.

To join the field and play your instrument in the Unique Self Symphony, you must be willing to take your Unique Risk.

Your Unique Risk is always something that you can easily, in the public realm, get away with not doing.

Only you know that it's there to be answered.

You access your Unique Risk through deep listening in the quiet, through prayer, or through asking a group of close friends, who know you well, what it might be.

We're accountable in life for one thing only: did we take our Unique Risk that all of Reality needs us to take?

You don't take your Unique Risk once; you take your Unique Risk every day.

Our Code is about accessing your Unique Risk to be and live the deepest configuration of intimacy and desire.

Your Unique Risk is evolution living in you, as you, and through you.

THE WHEEL OF CO-CREATION 2.0

Let's take a look for a second at The Wheel of Co-Creation.

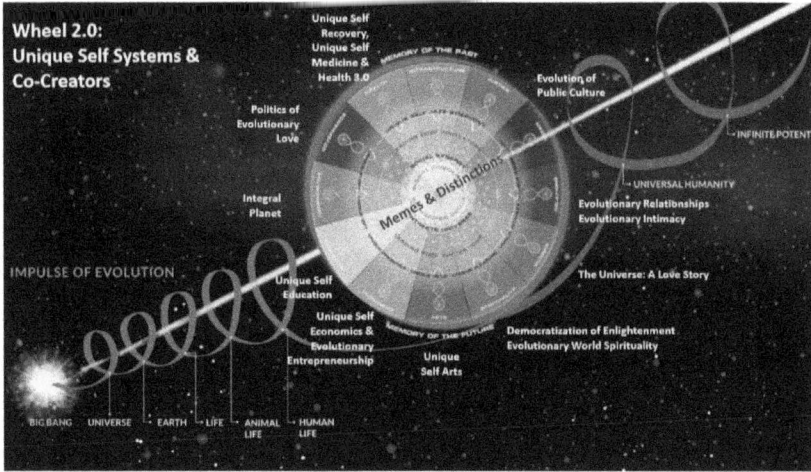

This is The Wheel of Co-Creation 2.0 that I actually wrote on a napkin, while having lunch with Barbara in Portland. Barbara had done Wheel 1.0, and this was our merging of memes. We agreed that the Wheel 2.0 is the Wheel going forward. I've spent many hours talking to beloved Barbara, as she would share with me deep ideas moving in her heart, and I would share with her deep ideas and memes moving in my heart. Together we joined genius.

What we did is placed desire at what we call the heart of the hub of the Wheel. If you take a look at the Wheel: **at the heart of the hub of the Wheel, it says heart's desire**. I said to Barbara that actually, this is the prism of revelation. You should have seen Barbara jump out of her seat. It was part of Barbara's great genius, her capacity to get excited about the *dharma* as it evolved. She came to us in the last five years of her life because she said: "Oh my God, it's moving here, it's evolving here. It's alive here. It's awake here. I want to be here with you." We came together and we shared so much with each other.

I want to step into this place, let's start from right here. At the heart of the hub of the Wheel is heart's desire. That means that **desire is not local.** There is no local desire anywhere in the world. Desire is always part of the Field of Desire. What we begin to realize is that:

My deepest heart's desire is the desire of the Divine.

It's the rapture of Divinity. It's God/Goddess's desire, living in me, as me, and through me. Until I access my deepest heart's desire, I'm actually not aligned with my longing. I want to live aligned with my longing, and I have an inconsolable longing to overcome the crisis of desire in my life, to feel the pulsing and throbbing tumescent explosion of desire as the core quality of my life.

We've exiled desire. We say desire only lives in sexuality, at a very narrow moment in time, with one narrow person, and it feels a particular way, and then it goes away. Then we spend the rest of our lives yearning to recover that fleeting moment of desire, which we never do. Because desire always evolves. That's a mistake.

The sexual models Eros, it doesn't exhaust Eros. Desire lives in a billion points of light. Desire lives in my creativity. Desire lives in my innovation. If I'm with my romantic partner, desire lives as I kiss my romantic partner's shoulder for an hour. Desire doesn't only live in a particular kind of sexuality; it lives in *every* kind of touching.

- It lives when we touch our friend's heart.
- It lives when we touch nature.
- It lives when Goddess and God touch us through nature.
- Desire lives every place and everywhere.

When you realize the dignity and the divinity of desire, your life becomes whole. You realize that not only is there dignity and divinity in desire but that desire is ultimately unique; desire is never the same.

---

*You are a unique configuration
of desire, and your ultimate
desire is for intimacy.*

I want to make deeper contact, and I want to explode my desire into my unique creativity, which is my unique gift, my unique word, my unique voice, my unique incarnation. It's the unique way of being, loving, laughing, and living in the world, that's mine and mine alone. My unique configuration of desire is evolution's desire. It's God's and Goddess's desire, awakening in me, as me, and through me.

When I'm in my desire, I don't have an answer to the meaning of life, because there's no question. Desire doesn't answer the question of the meaning of life. **When I'm living my heart's desire, when I've accessed my deepest heart's desire, when I'm willing to take the lid off and go all the way in this lifetime—living, being, giving, speaking, creating, from within my deepest heart's desire—then I'm a prophet.**

The prophet accesses desire. You cannot be a prophet unless you access desire.

We have an image of a prophet which is mistaken. The great mystics say the prophet is *Bat Me'lech:* the daughter of the King, meaning the Goddess. The prophet is the "Candle in The Wind," as Elton John sang for Diana after she passed. She was accessing a glimmering or a shard of the Goddess, but couldn't quite get there because she couldn't clarify. But we felt her yearning. There were moments when she could find it. When she was working with kids and working with the oppressed, there were moments where she came alive and she could find it. But Diana was the ordinary human being who was finding the princess; the candle in the wind.

But we're all a candle in the wind. We all have a unique deepest heart's desire. **We're all royalty.** We're all sons and daughters of kings and queens, princes and princesses. But it's not a metaphor. Reality manifested the notion of loyalty in order to actually indicate—to point towards, to reveal, to disclose—the inner nature of the human being. But we exiled royalty to a couple of people: to a man and a woman, their kids, and their bloodline.

But we are all of the bloodline of loyalty.

- We are all Mary Magdalene.
- We are all Christ.
- We are all Buddha.
- We're all in the Buddha field.
- We're all Lao Tzu.
- We're all Moses.

We say in the Aramaic, *it Moshe bekhol dara*: Moses lives in every person, in every voice, and in every generation.

But to get there, *you've got to be willing to do the heroic, audacious, fierce, quiveringly tender, joyful work, the gorgeous play of clarifying your heart's desire and knowing your true desire.*

Because there's also pseudo-desire, there's pseudo-eros. There's desire that actually takes us off in a way and alienates us. When we're alienated from our longing, from our desire, then we fall into the emptiness and we seek to cover it over with every form of pseudo-desire. But when we clarify our true heart's desire, when we can actually speak our deepest heart's desire, then for the first time we can take our Unique Risk.

To be a prophet is to take your Unique Risk.

The prophet speaks truth to power. The prophet speaks truth in the places where truth can't be spoken.

The prophet doesn't hide behind the petty fig leaves of political correctness.

The prophet doesn't hide behind the petty fig leaves of fundamentalism.

The prophet doesn't hide behind the fig leaves of ego disguised in all of her distressing disguises.

The prophet is egoless. The prophet is Unique Self. The prophet is exploding with desire.

So are we willing to be prophets?

Are we willing to clarify our heart's desire to be Goddess's desire?

CHAPTER FOUR

EVERY PLACE I'VE BEEN
I NEEDED TO BE

Episode 161 — November 9, 2019

THE NEW STORY: I'M A UNIQUE CONFIGURATION OF EVOLUTIONARY LOVE

It is beyond awesome to be here, and beyond momentous. We are delighted and in joy, and we are trembling before God. There's a quivering excitement, a quivering tenderness, a quivering audacity.

Who are we? We are committed as One Church—One Church, One Synagogue, One Mosque, One World—Many Paths, One Mountain. We're at a particular point in history, and we call this the da Vinci moment. When da Vinci is sitting in Florence, with about a thousand friends around Italy, and they're facing the immense tragedy of the Black Death that had ravaged Europe, they understand that they can't speak the old hollow words; they can't repeat the old formulas. **They need to speak a new truth into Reality. They understand that a new story needs to be told in order to transform and bring new possibility into the world.**

So they tell the story of modernity, which is the story of human rights, the story of the emergence of the feminine, and the story of the scientific method. It's an emergent, gorgeous story with many shadows, but with enormous light.

That light changed and transformed Reality. That's the story of modernity.

But the story was insufficient. It lost touch with its deeper mooring. It didn't understand how to integrate spirit and ethos into the new Eros of technology. We literalized imagination in exterior technologies, but we forgot to literalize imagination in new interior technologies.

- We didn't tell a new story of who the human being is, what the human being breathes, and what our deepest yearnings were.
- We didn't create a new narrative of identity.
- We didn't create a story of power.
- We didn't create a new Universe Story.

Our exterior imagination ran away and literalized itself in all sorts of forms of gorgeous technology, but they lost touch with the deeper sense of what the core of a human being is. We got really good at facial recognition, but we're no longer sitting face-to-face. We got really good at Facebook, but we lost touch with what friendship really is. We got really good at connecting and providing information, but we lost touch with truth.

Our information ecologies are broken. We don't know what's true anymore at the very core of society. We can't trust the sources that should provide that truth.

We made the word truth into a word that's no longer relevant. Oxford English Dictionary's 2016 word of the year is "post-truth."

We're at this moment in time, this da Vinci moment, where we stand at the brink of dystopia. Think *Hunger Games*. Think *Blade Runner*. Think California fires as the first scene in the dystopian movies we grew up on:

People without power, and people dying because their oxygen machine is not working. Pacific Gas & Electric Company in California is just one example: At the center of one of the wealthiest countries in the world, United States, there's such corruption in the system that PG&E failed to re-track its own infrastructure. When fires recently broke out all over the state, people were left for days—in a first-world country—without basic electricity.

All of a sudden, we begin to empathize and feel the pathos of a world. **We begin to understand that that's a minor level of suffering compared to the suffering happening all over the world.**

Actually, Steven Pinker is wrong—Steven Pinker, my dear friend, who talks about the world getting better. A lot is getting better, there's a lot of beauty and gorgeousness in the world. But there's also genuine suffering. There's more suffering in the world today than there was at any other time in history, simply because there are more people. There were half a billion people 200 years ago, now there are 7 billion and counting. If you now have twenty percent under the poverty line, oh my God!

We said last week, everyone's looking to be happy. But happy means: *I want to feel like my life matters. I want to know that I have a seat at the table. I want to know that my joy and my pain and my loneliness count. I want to know that there's a way to connect and experience myself as part of this larger story.*

We're here in this One Church to make a revolution. We're here to be Marxists, but not in the sense of Marxism versus capitalism—Marxists in the sense of radical revolution.

We've got to deconstruct what's not working and reconstruct a new world. The way to do that is to tell a new story.

But not a fanciful story, not a New Age story, not a channeled story. That's not enough. Of course, the American story is not going to get us home. We've got to channel a story from the inside *and* the outside.

We need the best of the sciences—the best of physics, the best of biochemistry; the best of systems theory, the best of complexity theory—with the best of all the strains of Buddhism, Judaism, Christianity, Confucianism, and all the native traditions. We have to weave it together in a seamless new story that we can tell anywhere in the world, a story that everyone is going to understand: *That's who I am. That's my story. I'm part of that. That which unites us is so much greater than that which divides us.*

We're telling of this new Evolutionary Story.

In the radical optimism that's going to emerge from this story, we understand that Reality is actually not a fact—Reality is a story. It's a love story, and its insides are lined with love. **The best of physics**—the interior physics and exterior physics—**lets us know that the world we are living in is so radically good. It so radically invites our partnership. We're so radically needed, and we can do this together.**

So here's our question. It's an easy question, and it's the hardest question in the world. You have to go deep inside to see if you can answer it. *Are we ready to be da Vinci in this generation? Are we ready to take our seat at the table? Are you ready to play a larger game?*

The next question is, *are you ready to participate in the evolution of love by telling the new story?* I'm ready with you, right here, and we're going to do this. **We're going to weave the new Universe Story, the new narrative of identity.**

What's our goal? I want to set our goal, our *telos*, our direction. Our goal is that there are a million people in Evolutionary Church, meaning there are Evolutionary Churches all over the country. That people will start Evolutionary Churches all over the world. That there are One Churches all over the world, and they're One Synagogues and One Mosques and One Atheist Centers. It doesn't matter what they're called.

All over the world, we see the movements of the new story. The new story—like democracy, which everyone thought was absurd a thousand years ago—becomes the story in which everyone understands: *I'm a Unique Self. I have a unique gift to give. I'm a unique configuration of Evolutionary Love.*

EVOLUTIONARY LOVE CODE: EVERY PLACE YOU'VE BEEN, YOU NEEDED TO BE

Every place you've been, you needed to be.

Tomorrow you can be someone you've never been before.

Reality needs your transformation.

The only slave-driver in the world is the belief that yesterday determines today.

Every place you've been, you needed to be. That's a huge sentence. That's our topic today. That's step one. Step two: *You can be someone today that you've never been before.* Newness is real; you can be a completely new person today.

I can actually become something new today. I can actually break the bonds of my history, and I can break free. What allows us to break through is love, but we're going to talk about what that means for real, and we're going to go deep inside.

The only slave driver in the world is the belief that yesterday determines today. All our yesterdays—we think—*determine us*, and we can't break free of their vortex. The only true oppressor is that false belief.

What we're going to see is that Reality moves towards new emergence, and new emergence is the emergence of the new. On the one hand, *every place I've been, I needed to be.* On the other hand, *I can be someplace entirely new today.* That's what the depths of the Code is about.

46

PRAYER: THE REALIZATION THAT THE FIELD OF INTELLIGENCE IS HOLDING ME

Let's first turn to prayer before we go deeper into our Code. What is prayer? Prayer is turning to God. Yes, God lives in the One Church. But of course, the god you don't believe in doesn't exist. God is the Infinity of Intimacy that knows our name. God lives in me. **I'm both inherent to God, and God is inherent to me.** *Tat tvam asi*: *Thou art That.* But that's not all— that's just one dimension: the Divine that lives and breathes in me, as me, and through me.

God is also the force of what we call Evolutionary Love or Outrageous Love. It's the love, Dante says, *that moves the Sun and other stars.* Or Tagore: *Love is not mere human sentiment, but the pulsing heart of existence itself.* **It's that love that the mystics called** *the love before creation.*

It's the love, the impulses that birthed Reality and inhere in the forces of physics: the strong and the weak nuclear, the electromagnetic, and the gravitational—all the four forces are animated by Eros.

It's the Eros that drives Reality, what Stuart Kauffman calls the inherent ceaseless creativity of Cosmos—and, we add, animated by Eros and love. That's a second dimension of God; that's God in the third person. It's the God that's moving through Reality.

But there's also God in the second person. **The God in the second person is my intimate Beloved**; my intimate mother, my father, my lover, my son, my daughter, my brother, my sister. It's all of the dimensions of I-Thou, of you and me. It's the God who holds us when we fall. Every place we fall, we fall into Her hands. When Rumi says *let me fall into the arms of the Beloved*, he's talking about the Infinity of Intimacy that knows his name.

How does prayer work? The same way I can hear you talking, because my intelligence hears you talking—my ears are the physical instrument, but they're just a physical expression of my consciousness and my intelligence; my consciousness and intelligence can hear you talking. But my intelligence and my consciousness are not separate from the field. The same way I can hear you, the Field of LoveIntelligence—the Field of LoveBeauty, the Field of LoveDesire—can hear you when you pray. This is the deepest understanding of the interior sciences, and is now being validated by the exterior sciences.

There are no words you ever speak which are unheard.

If you cut through all the theology, **prayer is simply the understanding that the Field of Intelligence is holding you, knows your name, and cares madly about every detail of your life.** That is the personal that's beyond the impersonal.

That's the second face of God.

That's *I am Thou.*

So we turn to that God, who knows every single one of us and loves us madly and desires us beyond imagination. We turn to that Infinite Personhood, and we say:

> *Oh my God, can I bring you everything?*
>
> *Can I share everything with you?*
>
> *Can I pour all of my yesterdays, and can you hold my yesterdays with me?*
>
> *Can you let me realize that every place I've been, I needed to be?*
>
> *Can I bring you my holy and broken Hallelujah? It's all Hallelujah.*
>
> *Even though it all went wrong, we stand before the Lord of Song, knowing every place I've been, I needed to be, that every detour I took is part of my destination.*

We turn to Leonard Cohen, we welcome him into Church, and we resonate this hymn.

Hallelujah, and we come to pray.

We come to pray to know that every place we've been, we needed to be, and that we can be new tomorrow.

We ask for everything. We turn to the God who's the Infinity of Intimacy that knows our name. Friends, we have to reclaim this relationship to God. We can't be in some liberal bastion that's lost touch with the deeper linings of Cosmos, detached from three-quarters of the world that has this direct relationship to God.

Yes, much of the world that has a direct relationship to God is lost in fundamentalism. **So we need to reclaim God at a higher level of consciousness.** But God is waiting to be our partner. God is reaching out His/Her hand and saying: *Partner with me in re-souling Reality and telling the Story.*

So first, we turn to God, and we ask for everything. Because prayer affirms the dignity of personal need. Let's just literally pray for everything. Let's feel it, *Hallelujah,* around the world.

Let's raise this. Let's weave this all together and lift it like a prayer to the sky.

EVERY PLACE I'VE BEEN, I NEEDED TO BE

Friends, we're going to dive into our Code now. *Every place I've been, I needed to be.* I want to ask everyone to try and feel that sentence. *Every detour is a destination.* In order to take my seat at the table of history and tell the new story, we have to know that it's true. So what's the new story?

The new story is that I am an irreducibly unique expression of the LoveIntelligence and LoveBeauty of All-That-Is.

The new story is that you know the answer to the question, *Who are you?*

Who are you? **You are an irreducibly unique expression of the LoveIntelligence and LoveBeauty that's the initiating and animating Eros and energy of All-That-Is, that lives in you, as you, and through you, that never was, is, or will be ever again, other than through you. As such, you have a unique gift to give that no one that ever was, is, or will be can give, other than you.**

You're not simply a separate self. You're actually a Unique Self. But you're more than a Unique Self. You're Unique Self in an evolutionary context. You're an Evolutionary Unique Self. You're not just *Homo sapiens*—you're *Homo amor*. The LoveIntelligence and LoveBeauty lives uniquely in me and uniquely in you. So when we come together as Unique Selves, we come together and we create a Unique Self Symphony.

THE SELF-ACTUALIZING COSMOS THAT MOVES US IS THE EVOLUTION OF INTIMACY

Reality, which has always been organizing separate parts to larger wholes, is ready at this moment between dystopia and utopia to emerge as something new: a new level of intimacy which we call evolutionary intimacy.

Evolutionary intimacy is the realization that every Unique Self has a unique instrument to play in the Unique Self Symphony.

The self-actualizing Cosmos that moves us *is actually the evolution of intimacy*. From atoms to molecules to cells, all allured together, seeking greater wholeness, more intimacy, deeper contact. This is the evolution of intimacy that leads all the way up the evolutionary chain to the emergence of Unique Selves coming together at this moment as the next expression of the self-organizing universe—as a Planetary Awakening in Love through Unique Self Symphonies. Evolutionary intimacy is the realization that *Re-*

ality needs my gift, and Reality needs my service; that *without my service and without my gift, something's fundamentally missing.*

It's not just a metaphor; it's not just a mythopoetic read. It's the nature of the realization of systems theory and complexity theory, and it's also the nature of the interior sciences of enlightenment:

I'm here because I am intended by Cosmos.

Every detail of my life was intended.

Every place I've been, I needed to be—in order to create the Reality of my life right now.

I AM GOD'S EVOLUTIONARY PARTNER

The second part of our code is: *The only slave driver in the world is that yesterday determines today.* Let's see if we can put the two together.

Everything that's happened in my life has brought me to this moment:

- Every tragedy and every triumph
- Every divorce and every disaster
- Every rough moment and every rapture
- Every gorgeousness and every "oh my God that was awful and horrible"
- Every betrayal and every piece of beauty

There's nothing that was an accident. Every place we've been, we needed to be, and we needed it to be that way in order that we be shaped and formed as the Unique Selves that we are at this very moment.

Every place we've been, we needed to be.

Let that sit in your body. It's a big sentence, I know it's not an easy sentence. *Every place I've been, I needed to be; nothing's left out.*

That moment of embracing every piece of the story:

- The right marriage and the wrong marriage
- The thing that fell apart
- The business that worked and the business that didn't
- The fall and the rise
- The holy and the broken *Hallelujah*

In order to become a revolutionary, in order to participate in the evolution of love, I've got to have that mad love of self, where I really understand that nothing is an accident; that every place I've been, I needed to be; no one's left out. That's hard; that's not easy. But if you can do this, you can break through, and you can break through for everyone in the world that can't find this, for everyone in the world that has a hard time writing that sentence. We're connected to the whole field.

Now, let's take it the next step. The next step is, *Reality needs my gift today.*

The weave of Reality is such that it has brought me to a place where I can give a gift that there's no way I possibly could have given otherwise.

Every betrayal, every decision that seemed wrong, and every detour is actually part of my destination, part of the intelligent Cosmos in my life. Reality needs my gift today, and the only slave driver is the belief that yesterday determined today.

Let's go the next step, and this is where we really get it. *I am God's evolutionary partner.* That is actually true. I am God's evolutionary partner *today*; that's the next step. It's not hyperbole or a mythopoetic reading.

- I'm a unique cellular structure.
- I'm a unique atomic structure.
- I'm a unique configuration of intimacy and desire.

Reality intended me—that's what Unique Self means. Reality desires me.

WE ARE ALLURED TO PLAY OUR PART IN THE SELF-ORGANIZING UNIVERSE

All of biochemistry—atoms, molecules, cells—are all forces of allurement. All of Reality is driven by allurement.

- Reality allured billions of times in order to manifest me, pouring desire into the manifestation of the irreducibly unique me.
- Reality chose me; I'm chosen, I've been chosen by Reality.
- Reality adores me.
- Reality is pouring breath into me, literally, in this moment. Literally in this moment in my body, my consciousness is connected to my body. I can say my hand is going to raise, and then my hand is going to raise. I'm this connected, interstellar, gorgeous allurement structure of thirty-seven trillion cells, billions and trillions of exponentialized quarks, all in a unique web of allurement.
- Reality needs me.
- Reality needs my service.
- Reality needs the whole thing.

That's the new story. That is the truth.

Imagine this image; this is the truth of science.

The universe self-organizes.

There's an inherent, ceaseless creativity called self-organization. Imagine an anthill. Every ant in the anthill knows exactly what to do. Imagine now, the ants have become conscious. Imagine a beehive. The queen bee is not running it; it runs because there is self-organization. Every ant passes other ants in the path, there's an exchange of pheromones, and every ant knows what to do.

So how does that work on the human level? How do human beings know what to do? How do we stop the top-down, command-and-control world of the old corporation and the old government, and begin to create a synergistic democracy, based on a self-organizing universe, leading to a Planetary Awakening in Love through Unique Self Symphonies?

It is a self-organization, in which **every human being and every group of human beings give their unique gifts at the local level, and begin to take charge and transform Reality**. We begin to take responsibility. How does that self-organizing universe happen? How does every one of us know what to do? We're not an anthill.

We know what to do because we're allured by our Unique Self.

This is so gorgeous, if you get this. The structure of allurement that creates the Unique Self Symphony is: I'm allured by my Unique Self, and my Unique Self knows exactly *what's mine to do*.

What's mine to do is to commit my Outrageous Acts of Love.

- Who am I? I'm a unique configuration of Outrageous Love.
- What does that mean? It means I'm an Outrageous Lover. That's who I am in my very essence. I'm a unique expression and configuration of LoveIntelligence.
- What does that mean I should be doing? I should be committing Outrageous Acts of Love.
- Which Outrageous Acts of Love? Which Outrageous Acts of Love are mine to commit.
- Which ones are those? The acts that are a function of my Unique Self.

Now imagine Evolutionary Churches all over the world, and we have this explosion of Unique Selves—as part of the self-organizing universe, bottom-up—committing Outrageous Acts of Love.

I have Outrageous Acts of Love to commit that no one that ever was, is, or will be can commit, other than me.

That's beyond imagination—it's shocking!

Here we go. I am an Outrageous Lover, and I have Outrageous Acts of Love to commit. So let's feel this in the space.

Avicii, you're my brother, you're my sister. *Hey, brother. Hey, sister.* We're going to commit Outrageous Acts of Love. We're going to be the Planetary Awakening in Love through Unique Self Symphonies. Avicii is going to come on now, and we're going to resonate this in song around the world. We're going to take the *dharma* into song, and we're going to feel this in ourselves and feel this blowing out to the whole planet.

MAKING MY CONTRIBUTION TO THE UNIQUE SELF SYMPHONY

Let's just go through the steps one more time so we can get this.

Step one: What's the nature of Reality, what's the new story? The new story is:

1. The Universe is a love story. That's the best science we know.
2. It's not ordinary love. It's Outrageous Love. It's the Evolutionary Love that moves it all.

Step two: Who am I? The Evolutionary Love and the Outrageous Love lives in me. So who am I? I am an Outrageous Lover.

Step three: What's mine to do? It's to make a contribution, it's to step up. It's to commit Outrageous Acts of Love.

Step four: What Outrageous Acts of Love are mine to commit today? Those that are a function of my Unique Self.

Step five: When I commit my Outrageous Acts of Love today, that Reality intended for me and that Reality needs me to do, I am playing my instrument in the Unique Self Symphony.

Step six: We create something new, a new emergence in the world. A newness that never existed before, which is a Planetary Awakening in Love through Unique Self Symphonies. That's the possibility. That's the Reality. That's the story. We do it by looking deeply into each other's eyes.

Are you ready for this revolution, friends? There are no easy words; there is no easy way to say it. We're halting. We're going to make a thousand mistakes. But we're going to contribute, and we're going to give everything we have. I know how hard some of you worked to come to church this morning. I had the same experience.

But this is our community.

This is our palace in time. This is our temple.

This is the revolution.

We are da Vinci. We have to tell this new story, and we're going to tell it accurately. We're going to tell it scientifically, and we're going to tell it based on the best principles of everything there is.

We want to know what love is, and we want to look at each other's eyes and say: *How could anyone ever tell you that you're anything less than beautiful? How could anyone ever tell you that you're anything less than whole?*

We want to invite people to come together all over the world. Imagine, every Saturday morning or every Sunday morning, people are in a One Church. Everyone goes to their own synagogue, their own church, and their own mosque—but there's a shared Story, a shared *dharma*.

That shared *dharma* is this new Story of the Universe: A Love Story. Each human being is a Unique Self, and each human being has a unique gift to give. We join together and we create a Unique Self Symphony. We move out of the top-down and we move to the bottom-up, in which every human being counts; no one is left out of the circle.

- That's the power.
- That's the joy.
- That's the story.

So as we finish today, let's just look into each other's eyes. We invite this chant as we look into each other's eyes. *How could anyone ever tell you that you are anything less than beautiful? How could anyone ever tell you that you are less than whole?*

CHAPTER FIVE

CONFESS YOUR BROKENNESS; CONFESS YOUR GREATNESS

Episode 162 — November 16, 2019

TELLING A NEW STORY: HUMAN BEINGS PARTICIPATE IN DIVINITY

Welcome, everyone. This is the moment where we set our intention. Our intention in this Church is a Planetary Awakening in Love through Unique Self Symphonies. That is an entire story.

Last night, I was reading a historian who writes about the emergence of language. About 150,000 years ago, *Homo sapiens* as we know them emerged on the planet. For about 80,000 years, *Homo sapiens* were just like chimpanzees and baboons; they didn't actually stand out in any way on the planet. We were part of the animal community. So what happened?

What emerged is this shocking explosion of language. What did language do? There are those who think that language was merely technical, and it allowed for the communication of information about hunting. Maybe. There are others who say that language allowed for gossip, i.e. for people to draw a little closer and to form deeper bonds of trust by knowing more about each other.

Maybe.

Actually, language does something far more profound.

Language allows human beings to tell a shared story.

Instead of just organizing 100–150 people, huge groups of human beings were able to self-organize and come together because they were able to gather around a shared story and a shared vision. God loves stories. Human beings organize around stories.

The writer I was reading, who has sold about 10 million books, has had an enormous impact on culture, and stands for the leading edge of intelligentsia in the world. But tragically, what he writes is cynical. He says, *Human beings organize around fictions; there are no Gods in the universe, it's merely human imagining.* His name is Yuval Harari, who wrote a book called *Sapiens*, and another called *Homo Deus*.

We're writing a book in response now, as an Evolutionary Church, called *Homo amor*. Because actually, Yuval, my dear and beloved friend, *there are Gods in the universe.*

Yes, God is a figment of the human imagination. But the human imagination is a figment of God. Our human imaginings are divine imaginations. Human beings participate in Divinity.

We are able, with all of our vulnerability and all of our fragility, to find a divine human greatness. We are unique expressions of Infinity. Infinity loved finitude, and disclosed Herself in us, as us, and through us. **We are held by the Divine in every moment. We are God's partners, and we are divine miniatures at the same time.**

That's not a fanciful idea. That is the deepest realization of the human intuition of the interior sciences that we have. This is the best validated information of human beings doing the deepest practice of interior science and accessing the interior face of the Cosmos. Human imaginings need to be clarified. **We need to clarify our ability to access the interior face of the Cosmos, and we need to tell a better story.**

MODERNITY: THE WIN/LOSE SUCCESS STORY

At each stage of history, we told the best story we could tell at that stage of history. But these stories—gorgeous as they were, holy as they were—were also limited; they were too narrow. They were ethnocentric; they were just about *my people and my tribe.*

Then we finally broke through in the Renaissance, and we were able to tell a bigger story. We were able to move beyond the premodern ethnocentric perspective, and we told a modern story about universals, about shared languages of meaning.

As we created our universals, we moved into modernity, and we started to tell a story about a separate self and separate parts.

Science talked about the notion that the universe is a machine made up of separate parts. Our theories of identity, our social sciences, talked about the human being as a separate self.

Now on the one hand, it was beautiful, because:

- I'm a separate self.
- I have dignity in and of myself.
- I'm not only deriving my dignity from the larger context of church or kingdom or tribe.
- I have my own unique dignity.

On the other hand, the separate self was separated from the larger context, from the larger field of existence, and from the larger systems of the universe.

That produced both the gorgeousness of modern technology—the human being stepped away from the church and began to create. If the universe was made of separate parts, each part could be specialized and analyzed, so modern science exploded—but at the same time, we created a universe of dissociation. **We created a script or a story that we call the "success story."**

The success story was animated by win/lose metrics: *I win, you lose.* It was about status and accumulation. It lost the notion that we have intrinsic dignity and adopted a kind of corrupt capitalist structure—capitalism isn't inherently corrupt, but some versions are—which says *you only have value when you've produced and been paid for it in a particular way.*

Human beings, in and of themselves, lost their intrinsic value. They lost their mooring in the Divine. We lost the realization that we were unique expressions of LoveIntelligence.

This win/lose metrics story drove us forward and created, not complex systems in which the parts are allured to each other—Nassim Taleb's distinction—but complicated systems that were vulnerable, in which the parts aren't intrinsically connected, in which financial meltdowns take place, in which we are not intimate with each other, and in which we can't feel each other.

These complicated systems then generated extraction models from the Earth, in which we took out from the Earth in seventy years what the Earth took billions of years to create. We have exponentially expanded the gap between the haves and the have-nots and replaced face-to-face interaction with artificial intelligence that isn't actually connected—it's only computational power, but it doesn't associate or align with the structures of allurement and intimacy that move all through Cosmos. A success story!

This success story has brought us to the brink of breakdown.

It has brought us to a level of existential risk (a risk to our very existence) that Reality has never before faced. We're vulnerable. There's something sick on Planet Earth.

We feel vulnerable, and we've got to confess our vulnerability.

CONFESSING OUR COLLECTIVE VULNERABILITY

One of the things we're going to do is *both a confession of vulnerability and a confession of greatness*. As we set our intention, I want to just begin with a collective confession of vulnerability. For the first time in human history, we are vulnerable not only to catastrophic suffering, but to existential suffering, to what we call the "second shock of existence."

The first shock was the realization that we each individually die. The second shock of existence is potential for collective death. The collective death of humanity is a genuine possibility.

How do we respond to existential risk?
There's only one way to respond. We respond
by deploying a new field of language, which
means we tell a new story.

Homo sapiens emerged 150,000 years ago, and for 80,000 years, *Homo sapiens* were just like everyone else. Then about 70,000 years ago, we learned to tell a story. When you tell a story, you can then organize around that story.

So we need to tell a new story. We need to move from the success story to the *Homo amor* story. We need to take all of the gorgeousness of high-tech, all of the gorgeousness of our new god-like powers. Because Barbara loved high-tech, and still loves high-tech wherever she is in her continuity of consciousness. I would always say to Barbara in our late-night conversations: "Barbara, let's take *Homo universalis*—which was Barbara's name for the high-tech vision of humanity—but let's not get lost in techno-optimism. Let's infuse *Homo universalis* with Evolutionary Love, with Outrageous Love, with *Homo amor*. Let's tell that new story together."

That's what this Church is about. It's about understanding that **only by laying down a new field of language, by telling a new story, can we effect a source code evolution**.

We now understand that Reality is systems within systems within systems. So how do you change the system? We can't do patchwork changes; we don't have enough time.

The only thing we can do is to do a source code change in the very nature of the entire system.

How do we do that? We download a new story—not a fanciful story, not a conjecture, not a made-up story—the best integration of premodern, modern, and postmodern wisdom that integrates all the parts in a larger whole greater than the sum of the parts: a new story.

It's the best story ever told: the story of *Homo amor*, and **this story is based in the realization that we're all vulnerable**. So we just confessed our collective vulnerability.

UNIQUE SELF SYMPHONIES: HUMAN BEINGS LOOKING AT EACH OTHER FROM THEIR PLACE OF VULNERABILITY

I confess in this moment, I feel terrible. I've got a fever. I've got chills running through my body. This morning, I thought, well, how can I cover up the fact I'm sick? Then I realized no, I've got to confess my vulnerability.

We can only confess our greatness, we can only be Homo amor, if we realize our vulnerability and our full fragility as human beings.

From the place of that broken heart, from that holy and broken *Hallelujah*, we break out with the glory of our greatness as divine miniatures. That's the new story. That's *Homo amor*.

Our intention is a Planetary Awakening in Love through Unique Self Symphonies, in which every human being plays their instrument, gives their gift, commits their Acts of Outrageous Love, and we then self-organize.

It's a self-organizing universe. An anthill is an unconscious self-organizing super-organism. Cheetahs and elephants can self-organize a little more flexibly, but only with close relatives.

Human beings can self-organize with huge numbers of people based on every human being following their unique allurement to give their unique gift. Then we join genius, and we give our gifts together. Then we unleash in the self-organizing universe Unique Self Symphonies, as synergies explode all over the world in Outrageous Love. Human beings commit Outrageous Acts of Love in this bottom-up emergence of *Homo amor*. It's not top-down. It's not a corporation, which is a legal fiction and has no body. It's real human beings, looking at each other from the place of their vulnerability.

I'm going to play you a clip to set the stage for our confession of vulnerability and our confession of greatness. This is a confession of vulnerability. I want to ask you to start writing little notes about your vulnerability. Where is the place where your heart is broken? From there, we'll move on to our greatness.

FROM THAT PLACE OF VULNERABILITY, WE CONFESS OUR GREATNESS

Our intention for this week is to confess our vulnerability—our place of breakdown, our broken heart—and from that place of vulnerability, to confess our greatness.

We're going to watch a clip about a man who was called the Black Elvis. In 1982, he was all the rage of America. His manager, Shep Gordon, was actually on our Board, a close friend of Kristina's. He was creating female-only Black Elvis concerts for Teddy Pendergrass all across America. Then Pendergrass had a car accident, and he broke down. He was driving with someone else. She got out of the car and walked away. He became a quadriplegic from the chest down: Black Elvis as a quadriplegic.

Three years later, after he's been devastated, he decides he's going to get up—Shep Gordon was there on stage with him at the Live Aid concert—to confess his vulnerability in front of 150,000 people for 1.5 billion viewers, to reach out and invite people to reach out and create a better world. To help set our intention today, in this special way, here's this confession of vulnerability by Teddy Pendergrass.

Oh my God! There he is, Black Elvis, three years later. He didn't actually want to go on stage that day. Shep was on stage saying to Teddy, *You've got to do it. We can only confess our greatness through our vulnerability.* **When we have chills and we can't quite think, when our natural energy is not there, we've got to reach deeper and find that place.**

I want to tell you the deepest thing. The world is filled with broken hearts, broken vessels, and broken people. But when we break, something breaks open. So we're going to go all the way today, in a Planetary Awakening in Love through Unique Self Symphonies—with chills and tears and laughter all the way.

EVOLUTIONARY LOVE CODE: THE ONLY SLAVE DRIVER IN THE WORLD IS THAT YESTERDAY DETERMINES TODAY

> Every place you've been you needed to be. Every detour takes you closer to your destination.
>
> The only slave driver in the world is the belief that yesterday determines today.
>
> Reality needs your gift today, and tomorrow you can be someone you've never been before.
>
> Reality needs your transformation.

Every place you've been, you needed to be. That's Teddy Pendergrass; that's vulnerability. *Every detour takes you closer to your destination.* You think it's a detour—it's not. **Every detour is part of our destination.**

Every place you've been, you needed to be. If you really understand Reality, you understand that Reality is a series of transformations. That's not made-up. That's the single best statement of evolutionary science there is. Reality is a series of transformations. So my transformation is not just "Marc." It's not that each of us only transforms in our separate-self world.

My transformation is the evolutionary impulse, literally.

This is the new story. My transformation is the leading-edge of evolution itself. And evolution is driven by Evolutionary Love. This is the new story, validated by the leading edges of physics and molecular biology and systems theory and the interior sciences: **evolution is driven by Eros.** All four fundamental forces of Cosmos—the strong and the weak nuclear, the electromagnetic, and the gravitational—are animated by Eros, by Evolutionary Love. I have to access my wounds and my brokenness, find my shadow

66

and find my breakdown. **Breakdown only becomes breakthrough when it's held in Evolutionary Love.** It's only when we hold our beloved in mad love that they can break through. It's only when we hold ourselves, madly loving ourselves, that we could find that place where breakdown becomes breakthrough.

My transformation is not my separate-self transformation. **My transformation is Reality transforming itself as love in me, as me, and through me.**

Reality needs my transformation, and the intelligent Cosmos organized my breakdown because my breakdown is part of the story. We didn't fall in the Garden of Eden because the divine plan messed up. The fall of Eden begins the story because breakdown always begins the story. *Only if we confess our vulnerability can we confess our greatness.*

That's the holy and the broken *Hallelujah.* That's why Leonard Cohen's song is our hymn. It's our hymn in Evolutionary Church because we're only going to have a Planetary Awakening in Love through Unique Self Symphonies when we bring high-tech and Evolutionary Love together.

High tech: our greatness.

Evolutionary Love: our Truth, Goodness, Beauty, and our vulnerability.

When that all comes together, we're going to create heaven on earth. But if that doesn't come together, there will be suffering we can't even imagine until we can get to the next cycle.

We're going to do this together. In Evolutionary Church, we are called. We feel the vocational arousal to not remain as *Homo sapiens,* but the fulfillment of *Homo sapiens* as *Homo amor.* **Just as *Homo sapiens*, 70,000 years ago, were able to spread and organize and raise the planet**—make the planet alive with consciousness, beauty, goodness, and gorgeousness, in a way that no other species was, by telling a new story—**at this moment between dystopia and utopia when we can access robotics and quantum computing and biotech and nanotech, we infuse it with Evolutionary Love; we bring our vulnerability together with our greatness, and we tell the new story.**

MY BROKENNESS AND MY GREATNESS ARE NOT SEPARATE IN ANY WAY

Let's confess our brokenness. **We can't stand for the evolution of love**—we can't say *Yes* to the question *are you ready to play a larger game and participate in the evolution of love?*—**unless we can confess our brokenness, and from there confess our greatness.** Here's the invitation. Our prayer is to write:

I confess my brokenness, I confess my greatness, and I hold them together.

Write them together because they're not separate in any way.

I confess my brokenness, and I confess my greatness. If you've written it out, write it again until you can actually feel it.

- ◆ I broke down.
- ◆ I did it wrong.
- ◆ It broke down on me.
- ◆ It was unjust.
- ◆ I couldn't handle it.
- ◆ I couldn't hold it.

Even though it all went wrong, I stand before the Lord of Song, with nothing on my lips but Hallelujah.

What does the word *Hallelujah* mean? We say it every week. *Hallelujah* means *hallel*: pristine praise. That's my greatness. But the very word *Hal-*

lelujah also means *holelut*: drunken intoxication, broken intoxication. So actually, the word *Hallelujah* itself means holy and broken *Hallelujah*.

Hallelujah itself means: *I confess my brokenness, and I confess my greatness.*

When you confess your vulnerability, you actually move through it to your greatness.

I'm going to tell you something completely wild, I promise you it's true. I started Church with a raging fever. I still have a raging fever, and I still have chills. But I feel great. I promise you, even with these symptoms I feel great because we poured love into each other, and I'm filled with energy and I'm filled with delight. So although I still have a fever, I am not my fever. It's become the fever of Outrageous Love.

Our vulnerability, our very breakdown itself becomes breakthrough.

We are the revolution. We are telling the best story ever told at this moment between utopia and dystopia.

Our intention is to find the newness in this moment of power, and to join genius and tell the best story ever told, to re-language Reality. Just like *Homo sapiens* languaged Reality 70,000 years ago, not—as my friend Yuval Harari says—with fictions, not because "there are no Gods in the universe," and not with "a human imagination that was a mere fantasy."

Instead, imagine Harry Potter. The interior love in Eros and magic. Have you ever studied mitosis and meiosis? Have you ever looked at a chlorophyll molecule? Do you understand the magic spells being cast by the inherent laws of interior and exterior science in every moment in the Cosmos? *Its insides are lined with love*, every second.

Our intention is to own the new story; to become a "strange attractor"—as a church, as a synagogue, as a mosque. As Barbara takes us inside now, imagine this Reality. It's not, as Yuval Harari says, "a figment of human imagination." It's knowing that our imagination is a figment of God. The word Adam means *adameh*: imagination.

Homo amor is *Homo imaginus.*

Your imagining is God's imagining because God imagines in me, as me, and through me.

So let's take the lid off of human imagination.

ACCESSING THE NEWNESS OF HOMO AMOR UNIVERSALIS

I [Barbara] want to become new myself, as an example of newness. I'll start out with how I got to be new in the first place, and how I think we can get to be new now, collectively, and personally.

The way I got to be new was when something really terrible happened on Earth: the United States dropped the bomb on Japan. All around me, everybody thought it was great. We were winning the war, and we had the power. I recognized that this could lead to the destruction of humanity, which then created a radical newness inside of me. I asked, *What's good about what's new in this power*? I found out that nobody knew. I asked the church, and I asked the President of the United States, *What do you think is the meaning of all this new power that's good?* Nobody knew! That was in 1945.

Let's jump back and ask the question again: *What's new in you and me?* We ask, first of all, because of the dangers the world is facing—not only thermonuclear war, which is still very possible, but climate change and all the other problems in every sector. **We stand here in the face of the destruction of our life support system, a situation we've never faced before. This means I ask the question again, what new does this crisis bring forth in you?** Barbara, Marc, everybody in this Church: what new is being brought forth in us as a species by facing the collective challenge of breakdown or breakthrough? That's the context.

Now I'm going to put a collective answer to what I think is new now, and then give a personal answer. The collective answer, I believe, that comes through 1945 and all the new powers and all the new dangers, is the emergence of a new species. I'm calling this new species, *Homo universalis*. So I want to integrate *Homo amor*, the person operating from radical love, with the radical powers of *Homo universalis*, as radical newness.

We can't be new personally, unless we see the collective body that we're in.

Homo amor and *Homo universalis* is the person filled with the radical impulse of love, who first of all has a spirituality—we've been calling it **evolutionary spirituality, where we are one with the spirit of evolution going somewhere**. It's not only "God is everywhere," but God in us is going *somewhere*, as us. And where is God going? He's going where God has always been going: to greater freedom, greater order, greater connection, and deeper personal love. This is a good direction to be going.

Then we ask, *Where are you going that is new, vocationally?* What is calling to me and you, and to the entire Church? We face a planetary crisis of devolution in our lifetime, even much more than we thought the atomic bomb was, and we face this incredible potential of being the next stage of evolution—both internally and externally—through vocation. So everybody's calling, everybody's impulse and vocation, is new, because you're in the next turn on the spiral.

So let's just all take a moment to ask, *What is your vocational newness*? Let's take the lid off the top of your vocation as part of *Homo universalis*, as part of *Homo amor*, facing either the devolution of your species or the evolution of your species—as you. Let's breathe into it.

My vocation, after I've taken the lid off the top of it, is to see the planetary awakening connecting on the noosphere, just like Teilhard saw, to be

71

what we consider to be the purpose of this Church: a Planetary Awakening in Love through a Unique Self Symphony. I'm taking that as my goal. So as members of this Church, what is your particular part? Mine might be telling the story and giving the invitation, but yours might be healing your parents. But we're all in the same context, and context is everything, as Teilhard says.

We're in the context of birthing the new species at a time of radical danger or radical breakthrough.

No species has ever had this privilege before, because this is exactly the time. It is new.

The next feature is, *innovations everywhere*. I've had a real deep insight about The Wheel of Co-Creation 2.0, and we have not fully done this in the Church. Imagine The Wheel of Co-Creation, our turn on the spiral, and you are in it with your unique impulse coming from the heart of the hub of the Wheel, and you as a frequency of the Unique Self Symphony filling the Wheel.

I don't mean that everybody on Earth is perfectly good and wants to do this. But I mean, **there's enough of us that are lovers who want to connect, co-create, and make an attractor for planet Earth that we've never had before**. So I'm saying *that's my vocation*, and I feel *it's the collective vocation of the Church*, each member contributing their own uniqueness through their own incarnation.

I'm adding to this, **the use of high technology with love**. Starting with the thermonuclear bomb being turned into an entirely new plan, which is laid out by my brother-in-law, Daniel Ellsberg, in his book, *The Doomsday Machine*. He has a plan to change the Doomsday Machine such that we release those weapons and use that power for the good. That's what our Church is up to.

Then we have **biotechnology**. Are we always going to be animals and humans dying unwillingly? Or are we to have extended life, dying and living by choice? Then let's take **robotics**. Is it terrible that we don't have to do what robots can do? Isn't it wonderful that we don't have to do repetitive things, that we are free to do unique things? Then we could add **quantum computing**, we could add the **global brain**, we could add the **global intelligence**. I want to celebrate the birth of the new species with the birth of the type of human that we are, being *Homo amor* within a new species.

Now let's take each member of the Church in the context of *Homo universalis*, *Homo amor*, in the crisis of birth in our lifetime. How many years could our Church take—let's say, over the next five years, ten years—to be an actual signal of this, with many other churches signaling? It's just like those early churches did when they believed in the resurrected Christ, signaling the next stage of evolution. That's what I see, and I see that we are right at the threshold, every one of us, of a radical newness personally.

Let's repeat the Code in this context, which is to say: *every place I've been, I needed to be.* You could say: every place that evolution has been, through all these billions of mass transformations and mass extinctions, to get us exactly right here—and **tomorrow, you can be someone you've never been before.**

What is it like if you are Homo amor and Homo universalis, with the powers that used to be attributed to gods, in an Evolutionary Church infusing us with the entire story of creation? That's where we are.

Does Reality need my transformation? Yes it does, *because everybody is unique*. It's like every cell of the physical body is unique and is needed to coalesce with the members of the body that it needs to be in—to make the eye, the ear, the nose, the whole thing.

So let's end with the idea of joining genius to create.

Let's end with the idea of co-creation.

Let's enter the open arena of the evolution of humanity, **joining genius in the most authentic passion that could possibly ever be felt by human individuals.**

CHAPTER SIX

MY UNIQUE TRANSFORMATION TRANSFORMS EVERYTHING

Episode 163 — November 23, 2019

ARE YOU WILLING TO PLAY A LARGER GAME? ARE YOU READY TO PARTICIPATE IN THE EVOLUTION OF LOVE?

We are here to be in and to stand in Evolutionary Love, in Revolutionary Love. We stand to evolve the source code, and to tell a new story. Because only telling a new story can take us home at this moment between dystopia and utopia. We tell a new story between us, and we tell a new story within us, and we come together as a band of Outrageous Lovers.

As we set the intention this week, I want to ask you: *are you willing to play a larger game?* That's the question. Do we have a *Yes* here? It's the *Yes* at the first moment of the Big Bang. **The Big Bang is a radical statement of** ***Yes*****; it's the affirmation of the Infinite that finitude (us, we're finitude), that this finite Reality is wildly valuable and wildly needed.** I want to get this for a second. What God/Goddess was saying, in the deepest interior sciences, is: *I, God, am going to become more through manifestation.* **God becomes more through us.** That's so radical, so shocking! That's what the *Yes* is.

Second question: *Are you ready to participate in the evolution of love*? Do we have a *Yes*? We're writing Evolutionary Love Codes. What I did every week for a couple of

years was I sat and wrote a code, and I sent it to Barbara. Then Barbara and I studied the Code, compared it to her *52 Codes*, and we worked together and we brought the code back to Church.

The Codes are *evolving* love codes. If you have a contribution and you say, let's change the code, whatever the reason for it—if you think we can adjust it this way, one word could change it, or maybe it needs this or that—then send in whatever your deep suggestion is. Receive the Code and go to the deepest part of yourself. You might have a story in which the code came alive in your life.

These love codes are Evolving Love Codes, Evolutionary Love Codes.

We want to create a *dharma*, which is our set of evolving, eternal truths, a set of shared stories. These are Codes that activate the whole thing.

WE'RE IN A DA VINCI MOMENT: WE NEED TO UPGRADE THE SOURCE CODE

We're at a phase shift in human history; we're in the source code phase shift. That's where it has to happen. So in this source code phase shift, **we need to evolve the source code by rewriting it**. The revolutionary act of One Church is to rewrite the source code—not with New Age declarations, and not with fundamentalist claims, but by integrating what we call *dharma*: the best of all of premodern thought, modern thought, and postmodern thought. We integrate and weave it together into a new *dharma*.

I just wanted to share this with you, so you get what our commitment is, all of us together. I mean, I have spent seventeen-eighteen hours a day on this, pretty much every day, for the last thirty or forty years. Barbara has also spent decades on this. **This is our full-on commitment.**

- ◆ Imagine we're in Florence.
- ◆ Imagine da Vinci.
- ◆ Imagine the Black Death that devastated Europe.

The only thing to do is to rewrite the story of humanity. In a pandemic like the Black Death, you can't go to every village and heal every person; you've got to rewrite the source code story. And the source-code story written in Florence was the source-code story of modernity.

Modernity brought great dignities and great beauties. But there were also flaws in the codes of modernity—which included flaws in the exterior science and flaws in the interior science—that **laid the seeds for the potential disaster of dystopia**, with its win/lose metrics, complicated systems, runaway growth, exponential extraction, and a failed series of cracked narratives.

Steven Pinker is a great thinker at Harvard, and a great collector of information. He wrote something amazing, quoted in a book by David Brooks called *The Second Mountain*, which my good friend Terry Nelson gave to me, and which I fell asleep while reading late last night. Steven Pinker says: "Neither I nor any other college professor I've ever met has any idea how to help a student find their soul, train their self, develop their self, or anything like that. None of that has anything to do with what we're doing here at College." Did you get that? **There is no training of the soul; there is no source code.**

The flaws in the source code are everything.

The flaws in the source code of modernity brought us to this place of potential dystopia and existential risk. So what we have to do is evolve the source code.

That's what Church is. So when we offer an Evolutionary Love Code, it's not like, *let's just have a nice time at Church*. No, we are here as revolutionaries. We are trembling before God.

So who are we? We are evolutionaries and revolutionaries, filled with Evolutionary Love, trembling before God. Just like the scribes of the ancient Torah Scroll would purify themselves in order to write the text, we have to actually purify our hearts, clean our shadows, transform our egos, to get so clean and so clear that we can together write this new source code, and then share the source code with Reality. **That changes Reality.** You think I'm making this up? It's the best of history and anthropology, and on this I agree with my friend, Yuval Harari: *Homo sapiens*, Chapter Two: **the only way you change Reality is you change the story**. That's what One Church is about.

So when we chant *Amor*, love, we're not saying it like we're singing a pretty song. This is not, as Hafiz the poet writes, *parading in pretty costumes*. What we're doing is we're saying *Amor*—not ordinary love, but Outrageous Love—**that's the source code of Reality**. These are the reasons why we want to share the Church with you, with all of us, with the world—**the right read of Reality is that it's a love story, and it's going somewhere.**

These are the plotlines of the story, and this is how we participate. That's what we're bringing down here together. So when we say *Amor*, that's our intention, and all of that is at play.

PRAYER: GOD IS THE INFINITE PERSONHOOD OF COSMOS

We turn to God, who is not only the Infinity of Power but the Infinity of Intimacy. I remember when that sentence first came down. Actually, I had a conversation that week with a woman named Cynthia Bourgeault, and she was like, *Wow, that captures my whole tradition.* God is the Infinity of Intimacy.

We live in an Intimate Universe, and the Intimate Universe lives in us, and the Intimate Universe is Source. But Source is not neutral. Source is not just pure *empty awareness*—the Buddhists caught that sense of empty awareness, but they didn't catch the inside of it which my Hindu friends caught: *Sat Chit Ananda. Sat* is being, *Chit* is consciousness, and *Ananda* is bliss, love, intimacy.

The Infinity of Intimacy desires Reality and births Reality, and the Infinity of Intimacy holds us in every moment.

- ◆ What that means is that God is not only the third-person power that moves through Reality.
- ◆ God is not just *Tat Tvam Asi*: God in the first person who lives in me, as me, and through me.
- ◆ God is also the God whom Rumi fell madly in love with. God is the Christ who holds me. God is also in the second person: the infinite Personhood of Cosmos.

If I just said, *I want to call you this week*, that's personal between me and you, but the personhood I hope will emerge between us when we call—that but *barely participates* in the infinite Personhood of God.

God is more than personal, but
God is not less than personal.

God knows my name. God is not less than the delightful quality of personhood in my most gorgeous moment of relationship—God is more than that.

God is the quality of the Infinity of Intimacy that knows my name and says:

I'm holding you in every second, and you're never alone.

God turns to us and says:

I want to hear everything.

I'm your Outrageous Lover.

Ask for everything.

I can't say Yes to everything, but I can hold every prayer, and my Yes is the Yes to your life.

So can you please tell me everything?

Can you share with me, please, your holy and your broken Hallelujah?

Just feel that for a second, *God holds my holy and my broken Hallelujah.*

The infinity of God who is all the laws of physics and chemistry, and the infinity of Cosmos, is sitting in a chair, looking at you, knowing your name.

That's the Infinity of Intimacy.

So we go and we pray. Leonard Cohen is with us, and he sings our chant: the holy and the broken *Hallelujah.*

As we say every week, *Hallelujah* literally means broken intoxication and pristine praise.

We did confession of vulnerability and confession of greatness, the two practices of our One Church, and they live together: our holy and our broken *Hallelujah.*

From that place, we turn to the Infinity of Intimacy, because prayer affirms the dignity of personal need, and we ask for everything.

- I am God's partner.
- I'm God's evolutionary partner. That's who I am in my core essence.
- *I'm God's whole mate.*

Let's lift these prayers to the sky together.

EVOLUTIONARY LOVE CODE: REALITY IS DRIVEN BY EROS

Reality is driven by Eros.

The interior feeling of Eros is pleasure, so we might also say Reality is driven by pleasure.

The highest pleasure is transformation, and transformation is the highest form of power.

Every human being is born to effect a unique personal transformation, and every human being is born to effect a unique social transformation.

Wisdom is knowing what is yours to transform and what is not.

The highest transformation is the transformation of everything, and the highest power is the power to transform everything which belongs to every single human being.

The highest knowing is to know that your radical commitment to your unique transformation is what transforms everything.

Reality is driven by Eros. The four fundamental forces: the strong and the weak nuclear, the electromagnetic, and the gravitational are all animated by something. Reality is not just a materialist, scientific fact. A materialist, scientific read of Reality is that *there is no story*. The classical religious read is a symbolic, mystical, mythical read that says: *the story of this Reality is not what's essential, this Reality is a symbol for moving beyond this Reality.*

There are three major reads of Reality.

1. One is the materialist read, that *there is no story*. You reduce Reality, you break it down to its smallest parts in a hadron collider. This is very important for certain kinds of information, but this view basically says *there's no story to Reality.*

2. The classical religions and perennial philosophy say that

the story of this Reality doesn't really matter. It's really about transcending this Reality into pure consciousness or into the symbolic interior psychological processes happening in you. We're saying, Yes, that's also important.

3. But we're taking a third step, and *we're actually realizing evolution.*

Even Einstein didn't quite understand evolution until he understood the formula. In 1914, the mathematics told him that *the universe is expanding.* So we actually realize, and evolution tells us:

◆ Reality is not a fact—it's a story. Stories have a plotline, and the plotline of the story is love.

◆ Reality is not an ordinary story. It's a love story.

◆ It's not an ordinary love story. It's an Evolutionary Love Story, driven by Eros.

Reality is driven by Evolutionary Love.

Now, what does Evolutionary Love feel like on the inside? Let's look at the next line of the Code. **The interior feeling of Eros is pleasure.**

When things break apart, it's fragmented, and it's painful; divorce is painful. **When we come together in the best sense**, in true union, in *hieros gamos*, the divine marriage that happens all the way up and all the way down, from the level of three quarks coming together in the first moments of the Big Bang, all the way up to atoms and molecules allured to each other—**the holy joining happens all the way up and all the way down**. That's a huge sentence.

What we're understanding is that **it's all driven by Eros, it's all a love story, and the interior feeling of love is pleasure**.

Eros feels like pleasure.

So when I come together with the split-off parts of myself, and when I come together with people that I've split from, when I don't call half of the country *a basket of deplorables* and split off half of the country—it is pleasurable. We've got to bring it together. We've got to find the beauty and *the shared story.*

TRANSFORMATION IS THE HIGHEST PLEASURE

Because the interior feeling of Eros is pleasure, we might say Reality is driven by pleasure. Now, are we talking about ice cream? Who thinks ice cream is pleasure? I do. I remember when I was six years old in Columbus, Ohio, and Baskin Robbins first opened. I was ecstatic—thirty-two flavors! So ice cream is a form of pleasure. But I have to cultivate my pleasures, and go much deeper than ice cream.

There are levels of pleasure, and **the highest pleasure is the pleasure of transformation.**

The entire thread of the love story—and this is the deepest science we have, both exterior sciences and interior science; this is a source code move—**is that Reality is a series of transformations.** That's what Reality is. That's true. That's not a mythopoetic read, a New Age declaration, or a fundamentalist claim.

Reality is a series of transformations driven by love, and those transformations are always moving towards higher love.

That's what it means to participate in the evolution of love.

I participate in the evolution of love by realizing that every human being is born to effect a unique personal transformation, and every human being is born to effect a unique social transformation.

Transformation is the highest form of power—there's enormous power in transformation. Every human being is born to effect a unique personal and a unique social transformation, and wisdom is knowing *what's yours to transform* and what's not. **The highest transformation is the transformation of everything.**

Let's track this together. Power is important. The highest power is not power *over*, and it's not even power *for*. It's the power *of* transformation, the power it takes to transform. **To be powerful is to transform**. Every single human being has a transformation that's theirs to do—that no one who ever was, is, or will be can do, other than them.

Every single person in this Church has a unique personal transformation and a unique social transformation. Now, here's something wild. Your unique personal transformation *is* a social transformation. When you transform what's yours to transform uniquely in your life:

- You open up a part of your heart that in the lineage of women in your family has never been opened.
- You transform a part of the masculine in you that in your entire circle, no one has ever transformed.
- You find your unique gift, and you give it to the people in your immediate circle in a way that no one in your family has ever done—and you transform yourself.
- You find yourself in that same cycle of collapse that you've been in your whole life, and you find a way to step beyond it, and you transform some dimension of who you are.

That's why we're excited to go to the gym. We go to the gym because we have a symbol, a visual way to see that *I can transform*. But the gym is just the exterior transformation.

I want to try and find the desire to transform in us. **The desire to transform is God-ness alive in me.**

Let's say the first thing: *I want to transform. I desire to transform.* Feel the raw desire, the raw yearning; you have to actually find it. Feel the rawness of it, feel the urgency of it.

- I want to transform.
- I want to be more.
- I want to be greater.
- I want to be more wondrous.
- I want to be filled with more love.
- I want to be filled with more possibility.

You've got to scream it.

It's an urgent scream of God/Goddess rising in me. **I want to transform!**

That's what it feels like. It's not just "pretty costumes." **It's this urgent, deep, bellowing, demanding, insistent force in me**—which I don't want to therapize away—that says, *I want to transform!* That is God, and it's beautiful and gorgeous. I want to listen to that voice because that is the prophet in me saying, *I want to transform.*

MY TRANSFORMATION TRANSFORMS EVERYTHING BECAUSE REALITY LIVES IN ME

So how do you find the power of transformation? It's knowing this: that *all of Reality lives in me.* You might think I just made that up. You might think that's just a New Age statement, or a fundamentalist statement. It's not. It's actually the essence of science today; it's the essence of the fractal principle of consciousness, and it's also the essence of the interior sciences. It's knowing that, on the one hand, I live in an Intimate Universe. On the other hand, *the realization of enlightenment is that everything lives in me.*

That's why we say in the great traditions, from a third-century Aramaic text, that *if someone saves one life, someone saves the life of the entire world.* We know it now in the leading edges of physics as well. This is what my friend Ervin Laszlo is writing about, what Jude Currivan is writing about—they're doing really beautiful work on this, as are lots of other people.

Here's the sentence—and you've got to get that this is true; this is where you get the power of transformation—**I know that my transformation transforms everything.** That's not narcissism. If you actually get the truth of that, that is a realization of enlightenment. Now, I also know that *your* transformation transforms everything, and I'm committed to serving your transformation. **But you've got to start with I.** I'm radically committed to your transformation, but first, I've got to realize, *I know that my transformation transforms everything*. It's a knowing that lives in me.

My transformation matters. My transformation matters ultimately to All-That-Is.

That is the realization.

This is what the interior scientists knew.

THAT WHICH IS ABOVE COMES FROM YOU

I want to read from a third-century Aramaic text that says, *Da ma l'ma'lah mim'cha*. That's an esoteric code found in the deepest texts that formed the esoteric Christian tradition, that formed Hebrew mysticism, that formed certain dimensions of Kashmir Shaivism. It's unbelievably beautiful. The text is normally read to mean: *know that which is above you*. But in fact, the mystics, in a hidden tradition, gave us the true reading, which I want to give to you. It's so beautiful.

Da ma l'ma'lah: **know that which is above**—*mim'cha*—**comes from you.**

That all of Reality, all that's above and all that's below—know that all of it depends on you. That's actually true. Your transformation transforms the whole thing, and my transformation transforms the whole thing.

To be an Outrageous Lover is not a simple declaration. To be an Outrageous Lover means that *I'm radically committed to my personal transformation in every moment, and that my personal transformation itself is also the highest social transformation.*

It's not that I'm stepping into a private hero's journey. **I'm taking my hero's journey for the sake of All-That-Is**. My personal transformation transforms the whole thing.

This is what communism skipped. Communism said, *the Unique Self doesn't matter; the irreducible gorgeousness of every individual journey doesn't matter, we're going to move things around only at the level of social transformation.* Communism wound up killing more people than any other single force in history because it was committed to transformation without this principle. We're now evolving the source code. We're writing a new source code where I realize that *my personal transformation transforms the whole thing.*

It's even more than that. When you actually realize, *who am I at my core?* Stay with me—I'll break out in tears because it's so beautiful. I promise you, I know the truth of this. Exterior sciences point towards it, and the interior sciences know this as the realization of enlightenment.

When we say I'm held by God, God holds me—that's Rumi held in the arms of the Beloved; that's one face of God. When we get the laws of physics, the codes of information, the codes of all of the exponential laws of mathematics, that's God in the third person. But God also lives in me—not in a clever way, it's actually a deep truth.

There's a unique dimension of Divinity that lives in me, that can only transform through me. So my transformation is the transformation of God.

I am God, transforming.

- That is a mystical truth.
- That is absolutely true.
- That is a realization.
- It's the core realization of Solomon.
- It's the realization of Luria.
- It's the realization that Teilhard de Chardin began to intuit.

I am God transforming. God didn't create the world just because it was a gift. God, the Infinity of Intimacy:

- Becomes more intimate through my intimacy
- Becomes more kind through my kindness
- Becomes more beautiful through my beauty.

Infinity loves finitude, and Infinity becomes more being; there's more being to come. That's what we mean when we say *Reality is a Story.* There's more to come, there's more God to come, and **I am the more God to come.**

I AM THE MORE GOD TO COME

Let's see if you can grab that sentence. It's not just "I am." Buddhism stops at "I am." That is the journey. It's when I expand into that and I realize the truth of that, that is the alteration and the transformation. I am God transforming, and **I am literally the more God to come.**

Here's the last sentence, and then we're going to do a chant together, with hearts open.

This is why we can say with absolute truth—not as narcissism, but as the truth of Reality—that **Reality needs my service. Reality needs *me*.**

It's not narcissism—it's the truth of who I am. In psychological terms, narcissism means, *I hate myself, and so I bloat to cover up my self-hatred.* But when I get that Reality needs me, that is actually the truth of who I am—but you know what? I also know that Reality needs *you*, and that's why I love you—**then we come together and we create a Unique Self Symphony**.

---

*Reality needs WE, and that is
a Planetary Awakening in Love
through Unique Self Symphonies.*

That's the *dharma*.

You know when I can trust you? I can trust you when you can look in my eyes and say to me, *Reality needs me*, then I trust you. I don't trust anyone who doesn't think they're needed by Reality. They don't take themselves seriously enough, they can't play as deeply as they can, and they can't be as beautiful as they truly are.

If you don't know Reality needs me also, and you can't say to me that *Reality needs you*, I can't trust you either. And if I can't come together with you and know that *Reality needs we*, that Reality needs us, then we can't do it.

But when we can come together, that is the beginning of the next step of the evolution of intimacy, which is evolutionary intimacy, a Planetary Awakening in Love through Unique Self Symphonies.

CHAPTER SEVEN

LOVING THE MOMENT OPEN: A NEW VISION OF UNIQUE SELF SYMPHONY

Episode 164 — November 30, 2019

JOINING GENIUS IN UNIQUE SELF SYMPHONIES TO TELL A NEW STORY

When we say "there's more God to come," we mean *God is not just eternal perfection. God is eternity, but God is also evolution.* God is the timeless time and the placeless place. **Eternity means not *everlasting time*; eternity means *in the moment right now*. You can step into the inside of Reality in which eternity lives—immediately.**

So God is pure consciousness—eternity. But God is also pulsing becoming. And God's pulsing becoming unfolds as you and me. Infinity unfolds as finitude, and finitude is you and me.

So friends, we're coming together. We're here in One Church: One Mountain, Many Paths, towards a politics of love, reclaiming love as religion. In this moment, my job, my privilege, my delight, my honor, my ecstasy, my seriousness, my gravitas—with all of my heart with you and your heart with me and our hearts together—is to set our intention.

What is our intention? Our intention is a Planetary Awakening in Outrageous Love through Unique Self Symphonies. What does that intention mean? We're at

this moment between dystopia and utopia, at a phase shift in human history. At this moment, like da Vinci in Florence, we are the new da Vinci saying, as da Vinci did in the Renaissance, *we can't heal all the tragedy in the world of premodernity by going to every village in Europe, because we can't get there. The plague is too much; the peril, the disaster, and the pain is too much.*

What can we do? How do we change it all? We're going to tell a new story, just like da Vinci did. **Da Vinci told the story of modernity, and we're telling the story of post-postmodernity.** It's a meta-modern story. We're telling a new Story of Value. Human beings understand that God, or Reality itself, loves story, and story is the source code of Reality. It's not story as a fanciful conjecture, but the best integration of the deepest wisdom we have.

In this new story, we understand that Reality is evolution. This means Reality is not a fact but a story. What kind of story? It's a love story. What kind of love story? It's an Outrageous Love Story. **What's the plotline of the story? The evolution of intimacy.**

What is the highest expression of the evolution of intimacy at this moment in time? It's the emergence of a new structure of intimacy, which are Unique Self Symphonies, in which each of us give our unique and gorgeous and stunning gift.

We come together and we give our gifts together. **We join not genes but genius.** We participate in an orgiastic explosion of heart love, where we're wildly creative, coming together to create the new *dharma*, new codes, new social projects.

We come together in a bottom-up—not top-down, like governments or big corporations— **grassroots explosion.** It's the self-organizing principle as expressed in an anthill, but in a way that's become conscious, as we are free and autonomous human beings allured to each other, linked in Outrageous Love. That structural model, that new configuration of intimacy—the Unique Self Symphony—is the orgiastic explosion of Outrageous Love that is creatively transforming the world from the bottom up. It's the only way it's going to happen. That's the only response to existential risk.

So what's our intention? This is the place I most like to be in the world. I'm so just beyond honored to be here. Here's the question: Are you ready to play a larger game? Is there a *Yes* here? Are you ready to participate? Are we, as a Unique Self Symphony, as a unique we, ready to participate in the evolution of love? Do we have a *Yes*? Let that *Yes* rip! Shout it out! Let's love this moment open like it's never been loved open before.

Are we ecstatic? Are we excited? Are we filled with gravitas? Are we responsible? We are. We're evangelists—but not premodern, fundamentalist evangelists.

We are the evangelists of the new word, of the new story. Evangelism means spreading the good news: the new information of the sciences, both interior and exterior. This is the gorgeous news.

COMING TOGETHER AS A BAND OF OUTRAGEOUS LOVERS TO LOVE THE MOMENT OPEN

Friends, when we say something is like a big mad kiss to your heart, what do we mean? I'll tell you a little holy secret, which is written deeply in the source code of Reality in the mystical traditions.

The mystical traditions write about what I would call an orgy of the heart.

Now, orgies of the body haven't worked that well in human history, and I've never participated in one, nor do I intend to. But **orgies of the heart are actually the great yearning of human history. It's yearning for silent empathy and touch.**

- We want to touch each other.
- We want to touch each other's hearts.
- We bleed into each other. We don't want to be untouchable.
- We want to find and kiss each other's hearts with mad desire, to liberate ourselves and all of Reality from a sense of alienation and loneliness, and to know the truth that we live in an Intimate Universe that cares madly for us, that knows our name, that knows our every gesture matters, that knows our every word is a caress, that every movement and flutter of our heart is either receiving or penetrating Reality.

Our intention is to love the moment open. Every word I speak either closes the moment or loves the moment open.

Its insides are lined with love. I am loving this moment open. That's it.

I am—but it's not just *I am.* In Buddhism, we stop with *I am.* In this new lineage of Unique Self and Unique Self Symphony, *I am loving this moment open.* That's what it is.

Sometimes we say—and I apologize, anyone, just relax with us for a second if the word is hard for you, but I'm going to use it anyways—*Fuck the moment open.* What do I mean by *Fuck the moment open*? What I mean is *sometimes you need the fierceness of that energy.* You love it open! The moment wants to be loved open by you, and the moment wants to be Fucked open by you, in the most beautifully fierce sense. Because when we take the Fuck out of love, then love becomes limp and flaccid. What it means is *the fierceness of Eros.* Love it open!

Then feel your power—as a woman, as a man, as transgender, however you incarnate in this world—and feel the fierceness of your desire. Feel your desire to actually love and Fuck Reality open. You have only one question in every moment you have to ask, and only one question you're ever held accountable for. What are we accountable for? If I count, I'm accountable. If I'm not accountable, it means I don't count. To count means I matter. I'm a Unique Self, I'm playing a unique instrument in the Unique Self Symphony, and that matters more than anything.

What am I accountable for? For one thing, and one thing only ever. Did I love this moment? Did I Fuck this moment open? Did I love it open all the way?

The realization is: *this moment needs me!* That's what's true. This moment needs me to love it open. This moment is my lover, my beloved.

What we're doing here in Church is a Planetary Awakening in Love through Unique Self Symphony. We're bringing down the incarnation of the Unique Self Symphony. Now we're doing it in Church, heart to heart. We're going to try and bring together and create together to actually become Unique Self Symphony. Funders are going to step up, and creators and writers will be brought in, as we take this Church the next step. As this Evolutionary Church grows, it exponentializes—literally, this is the vision—until there's a thousand Evolutionary Churches around the world. There's no reason in God/Goddess's Earth why that shouldn't be true. That the Evolutionary Church becomes a wave of love, and we have this explosion in China, in Asia, in Bangladesh, in India, in New Zealand, and in South America. But we begin to have Evolutionary Churches, and there's this bottom-up explosion.

What's an Evolutionary Church at its core? It's an orgy. But it's not an orgy of body. Again, those have a bad record in history. In other words, the great sport of loving is intimate. It's a deep intimate sport, and a large group doesn't quite work.

The coming together as a collective intelligence—a beehive that's awakened consciously, human beings autonomously allured by their Unique Self, choosing to love each other madly and to walk together as a band of Outrageous Lovers—is called in the lineage *chevra kadisha* in Aramaic. That was the vision already in the first century of the holy band; **the holy band that comes together and loves it open together. It's an orgy of the heart. That's what a Planetary Awakening in Love through Unique Self Symphony is.**

PRAYER: A HEART-ORGY WITH THE INFINITY OF POWER AND THE INFINITY OF INTIMACY

Friends, let's do a meditation to enter into prayer, to enter into the holy and the broken *Hallelujah*. I'm going to ask you to close your eyes. **We close our eyes because there are things we can see with our eyes open, and things we can only see in the practice of the interior sciences; truths we can only see and access with our eyes closed.**

Our eyes are closed, and we do a simple meditation. We envision, we imagine. It's true that God is a figment of our imagination. But our imagination is the figment of God. Al-Farabi, Avicenna, and others understood this greatly. Imagination is a faculty that allows us to access the interior face of the Cosmos. Einstein said that only imagination reveals physics; imagination and mathematics merge into one.

We close our eyes and we imagine what we call, based on the great traditions, "God in the third person." God in the third person is the laws of physics that come into being in the first moments and nanoseconds of the Big Bang, from the exponential energy that lives in Cosmos, and from the billions and billions and billions exponentialized of light years, and from the laws of chemistry and of biochemistry.

There are thousands and millions and billions of reactions taking place at the most microscopic scale of Reality, which are so unimaginably beautiful, so shudderingly complex beyond the capacity of all the supercomputers exponentialized. They're happening literally in this very moment, right now. The vastness, the intricacy, the beauty beyond imagination. Just take a look at butterflies and see the intricate beauty in each butterfly. Reality is a celebration; Reality intends celebration. Beauty and shades of color and light and goodness, and the breath of utter and radical delight—all of that is God in the third person: all the infinite power, all the supernovas, all the complexity, depth, and brilliance beyond exponentialized imagination.

All of that God in the third person is now sitting in a chair, looking directly at you—that's God in the second person—**desiring you, wanting to have a heart orgy with you, wanting to be penetrated by your love and to penetrate you with Her/His/Its ultimate love.** God is looking at you. This is God in the second person, knowing your name, knowing everything about every holy and broken *Hallelujah*, and saying:

> *Come to me, walk with me.*
>
> *I'm holding you. I'm your Beloved. I love you madly. I care about every detail.*
>
> *You're never alone, not even for a second. I'm closer than close.*
>
> *I'm always with you, never not, in this very second.*

In this moment we turn to that God in the second person, the infinite Personhood of the Divine that suffuses every quark in the intelligence and consciousness of Cosmos, that is not only third-person impersonal—it's supra-personal. It's the personal beyond the impersonal, the Infinity of Intimacy that knows our name.

Oh my God, we offer our prayer. We start with Leonard Cohen who speaks for us as we speak to She—She is what we call the Infinity of Intimacy—and we offer our holy and our broken *Hallelujah*.

96

Prayer affirms the dignity of personal need. The holy Baal Shem Tov, the master of the good name said: **When I pray, my life's on the line**. I'm in mad love, and I'm turning to my beloved saying: *I want everything. I ask for everything.*

Everything means what we named two years ago when we rewrote the Wheel of Co-Creation, *your deepest heart's desire.* So let's now find our deepest heart's desire.

We weave these prayers together and we lift them to the sky.

- We pray for everyone who's never prayed before.
- We pray for everyone whose heart is broken, and for the parts of our hearts that are broken.
- We pray for everyone who has never quite recovered from a betrayal.

To weave your heart together as Christ did, as Buddha did, because we're the Christ and we're the Buddha. It lives in us, we are it. It's a Unique Self Symphony. This is the democratization of enlightenment. **It's only a collective awakening, and it's only the democratization of greatness that can manifest in Unique Self Symphony for the next stage of All-That-Is.**

EVOLUTIONARY LOVE CODE: THE HIGHEST PLEASURE IS TRANSFORMATION, AND TRANSFORMATION IS THE HIGHEST FORM OF POWER

Reality is driven by Eros.

The interior feeling of Eros is pleasure, so we might also say Reality is driven by pleasure. The highest pleasure is transformation, and transformation is the highest form of power.

Every human being is born to effect a unique personal transformation, and every human being is born to effect a unique social transformation.

Wisdom is knowing what is yours to transform and what is not.

The highest transformation is the transformation of everything, and the highest power is the power to transform everything which belongs to every single human being.

The highest knowing is to know that your radical commitment to your unique transformation is what transforms everything.

The highest pleasure is transformation, and transformation is the highest form of power. We don't leave power out—**we want to be power-hungry.** *Homo amor*, the awakening of the new human and new humanity, with a shared story, with a shared set of codes that are the source code of Reality itself.

We're not against power, we love power. But it's not the dominance of power-over which is abusive, but power-over which is holy, because we all have power over each other. And it's also power-for, and the power of transformation. So we want to be power-hungry.

God is the infinity not only of intimacy, but of power. **Power is gorgeous. The elixir of power is awakened and alive. Feel your creative power.**

Every human being has power. *Every human being is born to effect a unique personal transformation, and every human being is born to effect a unique social transformation, and wisdom is knowing what's yours to transform and what's not.*

The highest transformation is the transformation of everything, and the highest power is the power to transform everything. It belongs not to the elite, and not just to Buddha under the Bodhi tree, but it's literally the democratization of enlightenment, available to every human being.

The highest knowing is to know that your commitment to your and our unique transformation is that which transforms everything.

FEEL A UNIQUE TRANSFORMATION THAT'S UNIQUELY PERSONAL AS YOU

We need to let the tears in the whole way, and leave nothing out when the tears come in. **They go exactly where they need to go and free you from exactly what you were holding on to before**. I don't know if it's because I let the tears in last week, or because of the timing on the planet. But this past week, something happened to me that I then wanted to go over for all of us.

I'm going to say that this particular Code, if you take it point by point, leads to the radical empowerment of that pleasure of transformation. This is actually a Code for achieving it. So when I started to go over it today, and after realizing what was happening to me, I realized that **everyone's transformational purpose is complex**. It's not just, for example, *I'd just like to get a great teaching job,* or *somebody is going to give me some money*, or blah, blah, blah. It's actually filled with complexity, and we need to get the necessary degree of power.

What is the power for? *It's the power to express and transform everything.* The reason we have to transform everything now, is that everything is going into dysfunction, in every field in the traditional mode. But on the other hand, there is also this rising up in every field, in every function, something that's working—and that's about to connect.

But what about in us personally? What about the fact that everything that has been challenging or difficult or threatening, we've responded to in this Church with love and faith and openness and clarity? We don't have to disguise to ourselves if we're feeling terrible. It's awful and we can't stand it, whatever it is. Then, having gone through that with the tears, let's go through this particular Code from the point of view of radical power.

What happened this week, and I won't go into any detail, is that about six or seven single things that we have been working on all started to happen simultaneously, all at once. Suddenly, it was a convergence of what's emergent. **Just like you can have a convergence leading to a terrible devolution in society, we also can have convergence of what's arising on the meta-scale, and on the personal scale,** just like we have here on this Code. So when I saw it happening, I realized how much of my life had been in these various paths, all of which looked to me like they wouldn't work.

Anyway, as I go through this, I want you to be holding the possibility that each one of these lines is going to give you somewhat of a trajectory, which then could go into a convergence of radical power for you personally, and then let's say for the Church, and then let's say for Eros in all of humanity. Because we might as well take it the whole way as we go down into the personal and the local. **Personal transformation leads to the radical transformation of the whole system.**

Because you can't be transformed personally without going the whole way, and your whole way is a microcosm of the planet's whole way. Here's a big statement, and we can write that one down:

Your personal transformation is a transformation in-person of the whole system.

This is because what it takes for you to transform is almost everything inside of you, which is generic for almost everybody. So we are each emerging as personal models for each other. The more we can share this in the Church, the more everybody can learn all the different things.

As I say, I don't know anybody who's old in the Church. My position is that **I don't like to call myself an elder, but a "newer." That is to say, the older you get the newer you get.** Why? Because evolution is always getting new, so you've had more of it than most. That's really true.

Reality is driven by pleasure, so let's all get in touch with the deepest pleasure that is driving your reality. It seems you can bring it to attention

and bring it down to the feeling level—what is the pleasure your reality is driven by? The highest pleasure is transformation.

So now let's imagine ourselves being transformed by our highest pleasure, and the transformation has to be uniquely our own. Can you imagine going the whole way for you personally? Every human being is born to effect a unique personal transformation.

I want you to join me in feeling the transformation that's uniquely personal as you.

That is to say, *What is the transformation that nobody else could have but you?* Let's dwell on this for a minute, with all the parts of it. Every human being is born to effect a unique personal transformation that is driven by pleasure.

What you begin to see here is:

- The goodness of God
- The goodness of the pattern of creation
- The divine process of creation

And once you catch hold of it, it gives you the incentive to go the whole way yourself—because it's driven by pleasure.

Every human being is born to effect not only a unique personal transformation, but a unique social transformation. Think now of how your personal transformation, whatever it is, driven by your deepest pleasure, is actually effecting a unique *social* transformation that only you can possibly do. So let's ask: **What is your greatest social transformation that's coming from your unique pleasure of transformation, that all the energy in your entire being is longing to achieve?**

Now, *wisdom is knowing what is yours to transform and what is not.* Has anybody ever tried to transform what is not yours to transform? Has anybody thought about that? I tried to transform a lot of things that weren't exactly mine to transform, like the Democratic Party. [*Barbara speaking*]

But why did I want to run for Vice President? I had something in me that I desperately wanted to say. I wanted give a speech to say the meaning of politics from a platform that was good enough to be heard—and it was. So you have to notice, if you're doing something that is yours to transform, it might be that what you're doing is your unique social transformation, but it may not be objectively what it looks like. Because it has to transform you by doing it, it then transforms the entire social pattern that you are in. That's why the vice presidency is a really good example. Everybody who knows anything about anything I've ever done now knows that democracy has to evolve.

THE HIGHEST PLEASURE IS TRANSFORMATION AND THE HIGHEST TRANSFORMATION IS POWER

I think it's going to evolve into the pattern of The Wheel 2.0 that Marc and I created, that we would like to offer and have talked about in the collective before. But I think it's a pattern we could put ourselves into in the Church, with our deepest heart's desire at the center of the Wheel. In other words, we have the pattern of the whole system here, and everybody is going to find exactly where they fit best. To use Jonas Salk's phrase: *It's not survival of the fittest, but survival of what fits best.*

The highest transformation is the transformation of everything. That's just exactly what I'm finding out. Because for any one of us to transform the whole way, we have antennae throughout the system, or we couldn't transform the whole way if the system was dying, or the system was going to hell in one way or the other. **The highest knowing is to know that your radical commitment to your unique transformation is what transforms everything.**

There are things that are not ours to transform, but working for our own transformation is not selfish—it is the true gift we can give to God.

Now, *the highest transformation is basically the highest form of power.* When you actually experience the unique transformation that is yours and only

102

yours to do, when you are personally transforming, **your power becomes the power of the system itself through you**. Because you couldn't transform the whole way unless you were connected up to the system. I mean, I think it's a real truth that none of us could go the whole way unless we were systemically part of the living system, and that the living system is affected completely and totally—that it's an awesome Reality if that's true. And I absolutely think that's true.

So I'm just going to end this by saying that the highest pleasure is transformation and the highest transformation is power.

If we're going for power for love, we're going for power for Eros. That's what we're achieving together, folks!

The power of love is the power of the unique transformation of every person going the whole way in this lifetime.

CHAPTER EIGHT

TAPPED ON THE SHOULDER: THE RADICAL SHOCK OF BEING PERSONALLY RECOGNIZED BY COSMOS

Episode 214 — November 15, 2020

EVOLUTIONARY LOVE CODE: THE THREE FACES OF THE INFINITE INTIMATE

The god you don't believe in does not exist.

God is not only, as She has been described by the great traditions, the Infinity of Power, but more profoundly, the Infinity of Intimacy.

God is the Infinity of Intimacy that desires finitude.

Prayer is intimate communion between the Divine and the human.

It is true that human beings participate in Divinity.

This is the first person of the Divine that lives as us.

It's no less true that we're held by Divinity in every moment.

Every time we fall, we fall into She.

This is the second person of the Divine.

Prayer is intimate communion between the Infinity of Intimacy and the intimacy of finitude.

Finally, Divinity is the force of Eros always seeking deeper coherence and wider intimacies, from quarks to culture and beyond.

This is the third person of Divinity.

What's the motive force of Reality? What drives Reality?

What drives Reality is this quality of intimacy, this quality of desire that stirs as mystery in the Infinite, the stirring of desire in the Infinite. And it's the desire for intimacy.

The interior sciences around the world—not speaking to each other but each entering, through the various methods, into the depth of the interior face of Cosmos through intensities of practice—disclose this Reality. If you want to know how they came up with it, I don't have enough time today to go into the ten major modalities of interior science investigation, but for now I'll give you just one that's wildly important.

In CosmoErotic Humanism—the name of the new set of First Values and First Principles that we're articulating—we call it *Anthro-Ontology*:

If you want to know the feeling of Cosmos on the inside of the inside, go into the inside of the inside of your very own self and locate that which animates and drives you; this immense and intense and unquenchable desire to be recognized, to be loved, to be seen—the desire to be intimate.

We look for intimacy in all sorts of ways. We look for status, so people will place their eyes on us, because then we'll feel the fragrance of what we're really looking for, which is intimacy. We'll be recognized. We'll be held in some way. We look for intimacy in all the wrong places.

105

But the core drive that animates our deepest depth is the desire to move:

- From loneliness to loving
- From separation to integration
- From alienation to union

We seek ever deeper experiences of mutuality of recognition, embrace, and union. **It's that quality that you in this very moment**—beloved friend, you can locate it in yourself—**participate in the interior of Cosmos where the Infinity of Intimacy quite literally desires relationship.**

The god you don't believe in doesn't exist. God is not a cosmic vending machine.

God is not only the Infinity of Power.
God is the Infinity of Intimacy.

Imagine what that means. Imagine your most intimate moment:

- Exponentialized in pleasure
- Exponentialized in depth
- Exponentialized in goodness
- Exponentialized in truth
- Exponentialized in beauty

Then you can get the barest fragrance of the Infinity of Intimacy.

If it feels dramatic, you're on the right track—Cosmos is dramatic.

There is nothing more dramatic in the immensity of its beauty and gorgeousness. We fall asleep, so we're waking up now. We're waking up to the realization of the immense gorgeousness of this all, the **Infinity of Intimacy.**

The Infinity of Intimacy that knows my name.

The Infinity of Intimacy is not only the third person forces of electromagnetism, the strong and the weak nuclear force, and the gravitational force, all of them animated by this force of Eros that we call the third person of Spirit—but actually there is a second-person of Spirit.

This quality of second person is the quality of Personhood that lives in Cosmos itself.

That's a very big deal, so let's feel into that truth.

Personhood is a quality of Cosmos. Personhood means that *there's a personal depth to Cosmos.*

- It's not just a vast cacophony of "its."
- It's not just a vast organized machine.
- It's not just a vast expression of inert, lifeless atoms that happen to be in perfect synchronized order.
- It's a living Universe.
- It's a living Cosmos.

But it's not just *alive.* In its quality of aliveness it also has a quality of *personhood.*

Now, again, if you want to access that quality of personhood, you can access it anthro-ontologically. Find it in yourself. Find the most personal moment you've ever had—sometimes the words "personal" and "intimate" become synonyms in our lives—when you felt *most seen* and *most recognized* and *most held* and *most able to pour your gifts in and have them received* and *most not alone* and *most at home in Reality.* You were overflowing with the pleasure and the personalness and the recognition of that encounter.

Imagine the president calls you up. It's right before the inauguration. He says, *Hey, I'd like to talk to you. I've been tracking you for a while and I know everything about you and I'd like to share with you some insight into your life.* He shares some insight, and then he says, *Now I want you to know that I really need your help, because without that quality that's you, that Jack-ness,*

I can't be president. I need your help. Will you help me? Will you partner with me? You're the only one who can do it.

- Do you feel desperate?
- Do you feel devastated?
- Do you ask, *What's the purpose of my life?*

No. **You're ecstatic because you've been *personally* addressed.**

But imagine it's not Joe Biden, because it's not Joe Biden, or it's not only Joe Biden—blessings to Joe Biden—but it's actually the personal face of Cosmos itself, the Queen of all queens and the King of all kings and the Beloved of all beloveds. The infinite personal quality of Cosmos is looking at you, loving you madly and saying, *Oh my God, I need you. Will you partner with me?*

Wow! That's the Infinity of Intimacy that knows your name.

It's to that Infinity of Intimacy that we turn in prayer:

- As beloveds
- As partners
- As madly devoted servants
- As subjects
- As infinite lovers

We desperately need to know that we're not alone. Need discloses the nature of Reality. Infinity needs our partnership. When we hold hands, when all of evolution is moving as us, animated by the Infinity of Intimacy, we can *do* anything, we can *change* anything, we can *transform* anything.

IN PRAYER WE TURN TO THE INFINITY OF INTIMACY THAT KNOWS OUR NAME

So we turn in this moment to God, to the Infinity of Intimacy that knows our name and we offer prayer, we offer our holy and our broken *Hallelujah.*

With every word we speak, we're desiring to heal the source code, to reclaim not the cosmic vending machine of prayer but **to re-soul Reality with the great partnership of prayer**. We want to deepen this understanding of prayer and this move towards God.

About a decade ago, I was talking to Cynthia Bourgeault, a lovely woman who's a good thinker in the Christian world. I shared with her this notion of God as the Infinity of Intimacy. I remember Cynthia saying to me, *I've been struggling to give this language my whole life and this is the language.*

God as the Infinity of Intimacy—let's just feel into that for a second. Feel into the Cosmos knowing you. There's nothing beyond that realization, to actually experience in this moment:

- That you are known.
- That you're seen
- That every detail, every jot and tittle of your life matters

That's not dogma or an assertion of some premodern fantasy; that's the quality and nature of Cosmos itself.

GOD KNOWS YOUR NAME

The names of the Divine are the source code of Cosmos. The names of God are the language of the interior sciences to describe the DNA of Reality. Now, the primary and most often used name of God, a common name for all the names, is *Hashem*.

What does *Hashem* mean? *Hashem* literally means "the name." God's name is "the name," because "the name" discloses Personhood. "The name" is not only impersonal, which was the major focus, for example, of classic Buddhist practices. "The name" is not only exterior laws of unparalleled magnificence, which is the focus of the exterior sciences. **"The name" is the quality of personhood that inheres in Cosmos. And "the name" knows my name.**

Let's see if we can just access this and find this.

- You're in Times Square in New York.
- You're in Piccadilly Circus in London.
- You're in one of the gorgeous plazas in Florence.
- You're walking on a crowded street in Dubai.
- You're somewhere in Africa or Asia.

You're in this big crowd. There are lots of people around you and you're feeling lonely. It's nighttime. Maybe it's a concert. Maybe it's a rally. There's ten thousand people around you.

We're actually going to do this practice right now. Locate yourself in your city. Locate yourself in that crowd. There you are in the crowd. There are lots of people. You don't recognize anyone around you. Lots of noise, lots of energy, lots of people. It's lonely there. You need to be there, but you feel alone.

Imagine, just now someone taps you on the shoulder and says, *Hey, Sally, it's great to see you.*

Wow! In that fleeting moment of being recognized and seen by an old friend, your loneliness disappears and you find yourself at home once again in Reality because your name has been spoken. Your name has been called.

The interior science of Reality, accessed across space and time, discloses this truth, which you can find in your own body, heart, mind, in your soma right now.

Reality is calling your name every second.

Do we often respond to that voice? *No, we're too busy doing spiritual practice. No time for that. We're too busy being holy. No time for that. We're too busy.* Whoa!

There's only one response to the calling of the name.

The first response is an overwhelming joy, just this explosion of joy. *I'm recognized*, and the experience of being recognized is joyous.

WE ALL EXPERIENCE SYSTEMATIC MISRECOGNITION

Every single one of us in our lives experiences systematic misrecognition. We're all systematically misrecognized. At the extreme end of systematic misrecognition is abuse and rape, but between the extreme end and being completely and fully recognized is most people's experience. We often feel that those closest to us are not attuned to us.

- They don't actually see us.
- They don't feel our beauty.
- They don't know our goodness.
- They don't know our yearning.

We're systematically misrecognized.

We're all systematically misrecognized until we locate the experience that *Reality itself in Her personal face knows our name*.

She is tapping us on the shoulder in that large, noisy, and boisterous crowd and saying, *Oh my God, it's so good to see you. I'm so happy to see you.* Can you feel that?

- This is the Inside of the Inside.
- This is *umka d'umka*.
- This is the Holiest of the Holy.
- This is the deepest of the deep.

Friends, this is literally the deepest of the deep: to know that **you're personally addressed by the infinite Personhood of Cosmos**, by the **Infinity of Intimacy** that knows your name and is madly delighted to see you and to recognize you.

In that moment, it all evaporates:

- All of the pain
- All of the trauma
- All of the contraction
- All of the loneliness of being systematically misrecognized

And I fall into the arms of She. Wow!

THE INFINITY OF INTIMACY WANTS TO KNOW EVERYTHING ABOUT YOU

Then when I feel deeper and listen deeper, I realize that that person tapping me on the shoulder has something else to say. That person tapping on our shoulder, speaking our name, then says, *How are you? Tell me everything. Tell me about your holy and your broken Hallelujah. Don't leave one word out. I want to know everything.* Can you imagine that?

I remember when I was fifteen years old I used to walk with Betty Ehrenkrantz to the Spuyten Duyvil train station in Riverdale. She was in a girls' high school, and I was in a boys' high school. We were Orthodox, so there was no physical contact between us, but we loved each other very deeply. We just took two or three walks like that. I remember them like they were today.

We would just share. We would just talk. It was the first time I felt the full experience of being called by my name, the full joy of recognizing and being recognized.

Marc, let's go down to the Spuyten Duyvil Bridge and let's talk.

Betty, that'd be awesome.

How are you?

How are you?

THE INFINITY OF INTIMACY SAYS: I NEED YOU

After we've talked with the Infinity of Intimacy that knows our name for hours upon hours, the Infinity of Intimacy turns to us and says:

- I need you.
- I know you need Me, but I've got to tell you something,
- I need you. I promise you, I need you. I love you so much. Every detail of your life matters to me so wildly and so infinitely.
- I love you so much and I need you. I can't do it without you.
- I need you by My side. I need us to be holding hands.
- I need to know that you're pouring your mad love and partnership into Me. I need to know that I can count on you and I promise you, you can count on Me.

Then you say to the Infinity of Intimacy: *Speak your prayer to me*—because in the interior sciences we know that just as we pray, the Infinity of Intimacy **also** prays—*speak your prayer, infinite God/Goddess, and I'll receive it, and I'll meet you on the Inside of the Inside.*

So Divinity speaks Her prayer, and you listen, and you receive that prayer, and you're willing to dare to step inside, to feel not only the infinite joy of Reality but also Her infinite pain and Her infinite sorrow. **You go inside. And by your radical audacity to step into divine joy, divine laughter, and divine tears, you liberate God/Goddess from loneliness.**

Then God/Goddess, the Infinity of Intimacy, says to you: *Thank you for receiving My prayer, thank you for receiving My divine holy and broken Hallelujah, and now let Me receive your prayer.*

And then you ask for everything. Because prayer affirms the dignity of personal need.

- There is no possible way, friends, that we can heal and transform this world by ourselves.

- And we cannot turn to God and say, *God, it's yours to do.*
- **We have to do it in partnership.**

Prayer is about the partnership between the finite and the Infinite, between the human being and the Infinity of Intimacy. Wow! In prayer, the human being initiates and invokes. In prophecy, God/Goddess initiates and invokes.

Let's download this knowing of divine personhood into the very source code of Cosmos.

We've lost our bearings. We've lost our moorings. We're stuck in visions of *the god you don't believe in. That god doesn't exist.*

- We have these false splits between exterior science and interior sciences.
- We have false splits between nations.
- We have false splits between different parts of ourselves.

We've got to return to the experience of knowing that we're fully held, but we're also fully recognized. We're known.

She's tapping us on the shoulder and saying: *Hey, let's go for a walk by the Spuyten Duyvil Bridge in Riverdale, and tell me everything.*

Can we do this together, friends, now? Let's finish by reading the Code again, together. Let's read it out loud with the intention to literally download this Code into the very source code of Reality itself.

The god you don't believe in does not exist.

God is not only, as She has been described by the great traditions, the Infinity of Power, but more profoundly, the Infinity of Intimacy.

114

God is the Infinity of Intimacy that desires finitude.

Prayer is intimate communion between the Divine and the human.

It is true that human beings participate in Divinity.

This is the first person of the Divine that lives as us.

It's no less true that we're held by Divinity in every moment.

Every time we fall, we fall into She. This is the second person of the Divine.

Prayer is intimate communion between the Infinity of Intimacy and the intimacy of finitude.

Finally, Divinity is the force of Eros always seeking deeper coherence and wider intimacies, from quarks to culture and beyond.

This is the third person of Divinity.

CHAPTER NINE

THE EXPERIENCE OF BEING PERSONALLY CALLED: A FUNDAMENTAL EXPERIENCE OF HOMO AMOR

Episode 217 — December 6, 2020

EVOLVING THE SOURCE CODE OF REALITY: THE FULFILLMENT OF HOMO SAPIENS IN HOMO AMOR

Welcome, everybody. What we're doing together is opening up new possibility. We're participating, literally, in what we call *evolving the source code*.

What we mean by source code is we don't want to have a nice experience, a little moment of inspiration, a little moment of sweetness. Sweetness and inspiration are gorgeous, but we actually want to be breathed in. **We want to breathe into, and breath in from, the source code—meaning the very core source code structures that themselves define Reality.** Those source code structures we call First Values and First Principles. First Values and First Principles are beyond time, they're beyond space, they're beyond which country you live in, beyond what period of history you live in.

They're that which lives underneath and animates, literally, everything.

The revolution is the initiation of a new human and a new humanity, the fulfillment of *Homo sapiens* in *Homo amor*. That's not some fanciful, wild idea; it's actually the interior narrative arc of Cosmos.

116

Cosmos begins with the Big Bang and matter explodes. Then we go through billions of years and then matter becomes life—that's the Second Big Bang. Then the world of life goes through all these stages of development, then explodes in the Third Big Bang: the emergence of the self-reflective human mind.

We think that's the end of the story, but it's not. There's what we call the Fourth Big Bang, this evolution of the source code of culture and consciousness that we're doing here together. The Fourth Big Bang is the emergence of this new human and this new humanity. Does everyone feel that? That's what it is—*Homo sapiens* becomes *Homo amor.* What are the qualities of *Homo amor?* What's the nature of *Homo amor?*

Homo amor is called by the future.

HOMO AMOR: BEING CALLED BY THE FUTURE, IN THE NOW AND BEYOND DEATH

Homo amor is beyond the void, *Homo amor* is beyond death.

If I'm called by the future, by definition I'm called by that which is beyond the void and beyond what seems to be the ultimate void of death. Because death has no future. That's how you know that death is not the end—because the human being is called by the future. **Hope always stands against death. Hope is not just some vague wish. Hope is *knowing* that death is not the end.** Hope is a memory of the future.

Homo amor is not tyrannized by the traumas of the past, though we do have to engage the traumas of the past.

But *Homo amor* is not just liberated from the past. My friend Eckhart Tolle talks about entering into "the Now." That's important, brother Eckhart, but the way you talk about "the Now," with total love, sweetheart, is you talk about it as if it's opposed to the past and the future.

That's a mistake.

117

> *"The Now" includes all of the future and all of the past. When we get that, we can feel the future in "the Now."*

In interior science, one of the ways we talk about the DNA codes of Reality is through what we call "the names of God." It's unbelievably important. **The names of God are interior science's language for the DNA of Reality all the way up and all the way down.**

The classical name of God has four letters, and the first letter is a future letter: *Yud*, Y, a future letter. Then the second three letters, which make up an HVH, or a *Heh, Vav, Heh,* in the original language. So it becomes Y-H-V-H. The *Heh, Vav, Heh* means, in Hebrew, the present, the Now. *Yud* means the future. **So the name of God is the future that lives in the present.** It's blowing my heart open.

Because I'm not limited by the present, death is not the end of the story but a night between two days. One of the reasons I know death is not the end is because death has no future and I'm called by the future. I'm called beyond the void of death, beyond the void of deadness that we can sometimes experience in this lifetime. We're called by the future. Literally, the DNA of Reality is the future calling us in the present, calling each one of us.

HOMO AMOR IS CALLED BY REALITY AS A REVOLUTIONARY TO IMAGINE THE NEW WORLD INTO EXISTENCE

We're going to be talking about the experience of the revolutionary. It's the experience of *Homo amor*. It's the experience of being called. **The experience of the "Call" is a fundamental experience of *Homo amor*.** *I'm called by Reality. I'm personally addressed by Reality.* It's a shocking truth.

As *Homo amor*, our commandment is "to imagine." Our imperative is to be Adam. The word Adam means "imagine." Adam includes Adam and Eve—they are one originally. Only later do they split into masculine and feminine—Adam means, in Hebrew, "imagine." We're *Homo imaginus*.

We're called as revolutionaries to imagine the new world into existence.

What we're doing here is we're loving each other madly. Not ordinary love but Outrageous Love, love that is the heart of existence itself.

We're awakening as Evolutionary Lovers.

We're awakening as Outrageous Lovers.

We know the only response to outrageous pain is Outrageous Love, and that the only response to outrageous beauty is Outrageous Love.

As Outrageous Lovers, as *Homo imaginus*, who's part and parcel of *Homo amor*, we're imagining the new Reality into existence.

Our intention is to play a larger game. With your permission I just ask you, gently, are you ready to play a larger game? "Yes, because we're badass."

- We're badass all the way.
- We're badass revolutionaries.
- We're badass humble.
- We're badass tender.
- We're badass fierce.

We're taking that quality of Outrageous Love, which is badass, to create and participate in the evolution of love. Just feel that energy:

- It's the energy of the trickster.
- It's the energy of the rogue.
- It's the energy not of the devil—it's from heaven, but it's devilish.
- It's audacious.

EVOLUTIONARY LOVE CODE: HEARING MY CALL

The human being is messenger of God.

That's what we mean when we say, "I am evolution."

I'm called by the LoveIntelligence of the Cosmos to be the messenger of God. There's nothing more tragic than to be a messenger who has forgotten Her message.

The deepest knowing is that my Unique Self, my soul's code, my body's knowing is the message. The message and the messenger are one.

Learning to discern the language of the call is the first step of awakening to *Homo amor*.

The second step is answering the call. To be called is to be personally addressed and needed by all that is. It is the source of all joy, Eros, and integrity.

The experience of the call is the experience of being personally addressed by All-That-Is. When do we feel in our lives personally addressed by All-That-Is? When we fall in love.

> *When you fall in love, you feel like the Cosmos is personally addressing you through your beloved.*

Can you feel that? Wow! *She knows my name.*

When you feel called, it's not just the experience that one person's falling in love with you; it's that **Reality itself is falling in love with you.** It is not just that you're falling in love with one person—which is gorgeous and beautiful—but you're actually falling in love with your call.

It's why people sometimes say, "Her work, or his work, is his mistress." And what they mean by that on the surface is that it takes up a lot of their time, but it's actually much deeper. What it means is *actually his work is his beloved, or her work is her beloved.* And when we say "work" here, we're not talking about going to work, as Dolly Parton sang, working nine to five. God, I just dated myself.

We're not talking about work. **Homo amor is called by the future. We're talking about vocation.** "Vocation" comes from *vocare* (voice), and voice is always before the content, it's the experience of being called.

Can I tell you something sweet that's coming up now? When you talk to someone on the phone and you haven't talked to them in a while, there's this first moment where you hear the quality of their voice. I have that experience often with people. In the original Hebrew, "voice" is the word *Kol*, and *Dibbur* is "the word" or "content." **When you really feel someone, you feel called to them and they feel called to you—it's beyond content.** It's not just about their *Dibbur*—their *Dibbur* is strategic. It's just what they say, the content: *Is it going well? Are we going to work it out? Is it not going well?*

But there's something that comes before that. When you call my name and I hear your voice calling my name, and I say, *Hineni*—"Here I am"—there's that notion of responding to the call, of hearing the call.

WHEN I ANSWER THE CALL, I EXPERIENCE REALITY BEING MADLY IN LOVE WITH ME

Step one is to discern the call, and step two is to answer the call. When I answer the call, I actually experience Reality being madly in love with me. And do you know why, friends? *Because that's what's actually happening.*

It's not grandeur or grandiosity. Otto Rank talks about how **psychology has denied our grandeur and, in doing so, created most of the complexes and neuroses and psychoses that it seeks to heal.** Otto Rank was a contemporary of Freud's and he talks about how this is implicit in psychology and therapy. Therapy is obviously a very important structure, but **within therapy there's a denial of human grandeur**. *That's your complex, that's your issue, that's your father issue, that's your mother project,* and it's always, *Let's go back to what your early stuff was,* and there's also a tendency to explain fantasy that way. "Oh, that's just a play of your early stuff." That's an important move, but it's not enough.

Dr. Kristina Kincaid, my partner, and I are working on a book on fantasy. One of the things we're trying to show is that fantasy is not just early conditioning, although it's good to look at that. Fantasy is your imagination. You're actually playing out, in your imagination, mythic possibilities.

When I'm called, it's not just my early stuff, it's not just my grandiosity. No. It's my true grandeur.

My grandeur, my greatness, is the true index of my real situation. That's actually who I am.

This is the most important evolutionary truth as we're trying to enact and become the new human and the new humanity—to realize that *I'm not merely a separate self.*

I am the discretion of infinity in a point of consciousness, which is Reality speaking through me, being me, or, said differently, Reality calling my name.

Literally, *va'yomer YHVH el'Avram,* "And Spirit spoke to Abraham." That's it. The content doesn't matter. Forget about the content. With total respect and love, it's what the Eastern traditions missed and often certain traditions limited to one person. No, it's not Mohammed, or Jesus, or Moses. *Eet Moshe Bechol Dara,* we say in Aramaic: "We're all Moses."

Literally to be alive is to experience the fact of the call, the fact of *vocare*. My voice is part of the divine voice. My voice sings a note in the melody of divinity. The world itself is off-tune if I'm not singing my note in the symphony. **My note in the symphony is desperately necessary for the symphony.**

Reality wants to be harmonic. Reality wants to be melodic. Reality wants to sing the music of the spheres. Reality needs me. Reality says, "*I love you madly. Please would you sing for me? Would you sing with me, please? Without you, I can't sing. I'm out of tune without you.*" Wow!

We need to sing together. Those we work closest with, we become a duet—*but we're beloveds together.* **We are quite literally the love symphony of Cosmos, and the experience of being called is the experience of Reality falling madly in love with us.**

So we're going to pray now. We're going to turn to prayer after we do *Amor*. *Amor* means its insides are lined with love, so it's the mad love of She for thee that calls you, and that is the interior truth of Reality. It's not fanciful, it's not a conjecture, and it's not a metaphor: it's the structure of Cosmos.

Amor, its insides are lined with love. Oh my God, take us inside.

IMAGINATION IS THE QUALITY OF THE PROPHET THAT ALLOWS US TO ACCESS REALITY

It's so important to reclaim prayer.

I want to read you something, if I can, that I got in my email this morning from a newsletter that's quite popular in liberal circles around America. I'm not going to say the name of the newsletter, but I just want to read you a little sentence in it because you get how important this prayer is. This very popular newsletter is talking about a lovely book by Thich Nhat Hanh, who's a wonderful man in his mid-90s, and he's doing a mantra, which is this practice of full-body focus.

Then it offers a line common in the New Age or liberal world. It talks about the beauty of doing a mantra, a concentrated and repeated statement. For example, "I am here for you" is one of Thich Nhat Hanh's mantras, which is very beautiful. Then the writer writes—this very well-recognized, well-respected writer: "Unlike a prayer, which channels a hope at some imagined entity capable of interceding in favor of that hope…" It's this casual statement that basically says: *prayer is ridiculous.* Ouch.

We've lost prayer. There's this arrogance in the liberal world, which presumes to read prayer out of existence because it's caricatured as turning to god as a cosmic vending machine.

> *God is an imagined entity, of course. God is a figment of our imagination. But our imagination is also a figment of God!*

In other words, imagination is a faculty of understanding. Albert Einstein writes, "I can't even begin to get the laws of physics unless I have the quality of imagination." Imagination is a quality of divinity. We are *Homo imaginus*—imagination lives in us. Imagination's not a child's toy; imagination is the quality of the prophet. It's a quality, a form of perception, and our imagination allows us to access Reality.

But it goes even deeper than that. Reality is *personal*; there's a Personhood to Cosmos.

THE PERSONHOOD OF COSMOS

This newsletter I just read from, which talks about prayer to an imagined entity, the cosmic vending machine, was talking about the god you don't believe in. And the god you don't believe in doesn't exist.

God is not an imagined entity.

I happen to like the word "God," but it's not the only word that we use. We can use Maat or Geist or Tao or Ātman is Brahman or *Adonai Elohim* or the Implicate Order, but God's a fine word. We have to release the baggage from words like God and Christ, and reclaim the depth of these words in a liberated way, because we have to create a shared, spiritual language in the world. Sixty percent of the world lives in a system in which God is central, and we all have different names for this force we call God.

But here's the key. **The key to the Godforce is that God is personal.**

God's not just an impersonal third-person force of physics. God is not just electromagnetism and gravity. Yes, the interior of electromagnetism and gravity is the force of allurement, which is a quality of the divine. That's the third person of God.

But there's a second person of the Divine, and that's Personhood.

- It's I-Thou.
- It's you and me.
- It's the Intimate Cosmos that knows my name.

This quality of divine Personhood is not fanciful. It's not imagined in the sense of a childish imagination; it's a quality that you stake your life on. It's the very deepest yearning of our deepest essence—transculturally, trans-historically:

- We live to love.
- We live to transcend loneliness.
- We live to be recognized.

That quality is not merely a human quality—it lives not just in the world of the self-reflective mind, the human being, but it lives in the world of life and the world of matter. There's an allurement between unique particles that, as it were, call each other's name.

There's an evolution of personhood, but personhood exists all the way up and all the way down the cosmological scale. I used a phrase a few weeks ago, talking to my dear friend and colleague, scientist Howard Bloom: *the personhood of protons.*

The quality of Reality is intimate. That's unbelievably important. When we turn to God, we're not turning to the cosmic vending machine. **We're talking and turning to the most intimate, infinite quality of Cosmos that appears also between you and me.**

Just as you can hear me talking, God can hear me talking. This is so because *you hearing me talking* participates in the Field of LoveIntelligence. You hear me because you're a discrete, unique expression of the Field of LoveIntelligence. If you can hear me, it means you're not separate from the Field. If you can hear me, obviously the Field can hear me. Wow!

We know that communication is actually not dependent just on ears and eyes. We know that we can have clairvoyance. There is validated empirical information for this. We can see without our eyes, we can hear from across the world without our ears—so there's clearly invisible lines of connection. That in you which hears me is the LoveIntelligence that we all participate in.

How could it be that you can hear me, but the Field of LoveIntelligence itself cannot? Of course the Field of LoveIntelligence hears me, and that's what prayer is all about. **I turn to that Field that knows my name and that loves me madly.**

PSYCHOLOGICAL STABILITY REQUIRES REALIZATION OF THE FUTURE BEYOND DEATH, AS WELL AS THE REALIZATION THAT I'M LIVING IN AN INTIMATE UNIVERSE THAT KNOWS MY NAME

I don't believe you can attain psychological stability without two things. One of them is something that Jung said, and the other is something I want to add to Jung. Jung talks about being unable to attain psychological maturity or stability without a knowledge of personal immortality, without knowing that actually, *I live beyond this world, that I live beyond the void, and that I'm called by the future beyond death.* If I don't know that, I can't actually achieve a stable sense of psychological integrity because the pain of entering into nothingness and having that all become meaningless is too much. So that's one. It's deep.

Second, *I can't achieve psychological stability unless I realize that I'm living in an Intimate Universe that knows my name.* If I experience the universe as being only pure chance, meaningless, and random—as opposed to that being one of many qualities of the universe, which it is—then I can't be psychologically stable.

If I don't experience the quality of symmetry, the quality of intention, the quality of beauty, the quality in which Reality is calling my name— I'm shattered. That's the experience of being called.

Wow! So when we turn to the Divine in prayer, we turn to the Divine because **Divinity is calling us, and we're calling Divinity, and we meet in the mutual call.**

That's what prayer is. That's what Leonard Cohen sings about in the holy and the broken *Hallelujah*. We bring before the Infinity of Intimacy that knows our name, our holy and our broken *Hallelujah*. Let's take us inside. Here we go.

Prayer affirms the dignity of personal need, so when we pray we ask for anything and everything: personal, intimate, cosmic, grand—it's all part of the holy and broken *Hallelujah*, which is the intention and need of Cosmos. But perhaps this week, friends, perhaps as we hold hands, perhaps we might pray to be able to hear the call, and to be able to answer the call.

There's nothing more narcissistic than to be so involved in my own daily emotional experience—*I'm angry, I'm sad, I'm up, I'm down*—that I don't respond to the call.

So let's hear the call, friends.

I HAVE THE POWER OF BLESSING AND I BLESS YOU

We all have the power of blessing. We've exiled blessing to the priests, to the rabbis, to the imams. We need to democratize of the power of enlightenment. **We each have the power of blessing.** There were years in Jerusalem where we would all go round saying, *I want to bless you. May I bless you? I'd like to bless you.* So let's bless each other.

It's not premodern blessing. It's not fundamentalist blessing. We might call it—using the language of development levels—*second tier*, or *second simplicity*. It comes from our deepest, highest, and most integrated self. All our rationality is included, and all of science. **The power of blessing transcends and includes all of it**.

Let's just take a moment now and bless each other, so that we each know, *I have the power of blessing, and I bless you.*

Feel the power of the blessing moving through you.

I have the power of blessing, and I bless you.

CHAPTER TEN

BECOMING THE EDGE THAT REDEFINES THE CENTER: REALITY IS BEGGING YOU TO BECOME A MASTER—TOWARDS THE DEMOCRATIZATION OF MASTERY

Episode 322 — December 12, 2022

HOW DO WE CHANGE THE CULTURE?

How do we now take this new story into our communities?

How do we take this into the world?

How do we share the truth:

- That Reality is not merely a fact, that Reality is a story?
- That Reality is a narrative arc, and that it has plotlines?
- That those plotlines are First Values and First Principles, and they're *evolving*?
- That your story is not just your narrow, separate-self story, but is chapter and verse in The Universe: A Love Story?

Oh my God! Our intention is revolution. But it's revolution that is *evolutionary*: the evolution of consciousness, and **the evolution of the very source code of love**:

- We love more intensely, and we love wider and deeper.
- We love with new capacities.
- We love the split-off parts of ourselves.
- We love the people we've split off from ourselves.
- **We *evolve* love itself—its intensity, its depth, its quality.**

And that love is not *just* cosmic, and it's not *just* personal. It's the cosmic and the personal *as one*.

That's what we mean by *Outrageous Love*—there is no split between the personal and the cosmic. **It is only this evolution of love, this deep knowing of what that means that will actually respond to the metacrisis.**

I want to invite everyone to something in a very deep way: We need to *study* the texts that we are preparing.

If you haven't read *Unique Self*, study *Unique Self*. When I say study *Unique Self*, I mean: know it deeply, and not just *intellectually*. Mind is one way we know—and we need mind, mind is real and important—but we've also got to know *carnally*; knowing is carnal.

- It's a carnal knowledge.
- It's a sensing.
- It's a feeling.

I've actually never *thought* of a good idea in my life, never, not once! And I promise you I'm not being cute or clever. **I've never *thought* of one good idea in my life.**

I've only ever *felt* an idea.

I could feel the idea in my body, and my body wouldn't rest, my feeling wouldn't rest until I could articulate that idea in a set of words, knowing full well that **the words are just holding the fragrance of the feeling that is literally living in the body.**

Through my body, I vision God.

DO THE WORK OF *READING*—SLOWLY, DEEPLY, EVERY DAY

I want to say—tenderly, but fiercely—that in order to make this revolution real, we have to create amongst ourselves *a group of us*. Let's call this group, *the ten thousand*. And in the 10,000, there's the 1,000, and in the 1,000, there's the 500, and in the 500, there's the 100, and in the 100, there's the 50, and in the 50, there's the 10. **These are groups that know this** *dharma* **sensually.**

Our sensemaking is sensual. We can feel it in our body, in our heart, and in our minds. I can feel it in my body and my soul—it moves in me.

But we've got to first do **the work of *reading***—don't skip the reading.

- Read *Unique Self* cover to cover.
- Read *A Return to Eros*.
- Go to the Unique Self website.
- Go to the gorgeous Office for the Future website.
- When it's ready, in about two months, go to the gorgeous new website. The Center for Integral Wisdom is changing its name, evolving its name to the Center for World Philosophy and Religion, and we're putting up this gorgeous website filled with deep pieces.
- You can go to my website, if you'd like, along the way.

We are generating a Great Library; we are working day and night on this Great Library. We are going to start putting it out in the spring, volume after volume—and I just beg you, with all my heart and soul, to ***read*, and read *slowly*, and read *deeply*, and read *every day* as part of your practice.**

We've lost reading as a practice.

Forget about the clips. Forget about the podcasts. Read!

Train your mind, and train your heart, and train your body, and through the texts actually *get* the *dharma*.

There is a direct relationship between *understanding* the First Principles and First Values and *working them through* in your mind.

- In the old world, there were a bunch of brilliant leaders, and everybody else followed. There was a very small group of people, the elite who did the sensemaking, and everyone else followed.
- Today, we need to be in a place where we are *all* doing sensemaking. **Part of the democratization of enlightenment is the democratization of sensemaking.**

Right now, we have so much information exploding on the web, a broken information ecology, a fundamental lack of trust in what used to be the legacy institutions, and the enormous confusion in the public spaces of information.

- On the one hand, we don't trust the legacy sources.
- On the other hand, the conspiracy sources are clearly warped and as broken as the legacy sources.

So how do you actually do sensemaking?

You have to first be grounded in a set of First Principles and First Values; you have to *understand* them, *feel* them, *know* them.

And so, I am inviting our inner circle, those of us who want to *be* this revolution, to become the new human and the new humanity: Read deeply, and then *feel* what you're reading.

You have to feel it in your body—**you have to feel the light moving in your body.**

ALL GENUINE KNOWING COMES FROM A DEEP FEELING OF THE LIVING UNIVERSE

Sensemaking is a sensual act—all knowledge is sensual. The word *knowing* is carnal: *to know* means to know *carnally*, to know *erotically*. I can feel you, you can feel me, and we've got to be able to *feel* ideas. **Ideas are *living* organisms**. An **idea is a *living field*.**

We think that an idea is just an intellectual abstraction, written in a book someplace. But *how* did it get written in a book?

- Someone *felt* something about Reality.
- Someone *tasted* something about Reality.
- Someone *tested* that tasting to make sure that it was accurate.
- Then someone shared what they tasted with other people and they said, *did you taste the same thing?* We began to get *validated* information.

I am not going to do a history of epistemology here, but **all genuine knowing comes from a deep feeling of the living Universe**, a feeling of a living Reality. An idea is not arid, abstract, dry, intellectual knowledge. If you think that, you don't understand knowing.

Knowing is sensual—it's alive, it's throbbing, it's pulsing, it's tumescent, it's dripping with life. That's what knowing is.

To know and to feel this new Story of Value that we are telling here, the story of CosmoErotic Humanism, is to read and to know. Reading is one of the ways that we know: we read, we feel, we are aroused to the text, and we feel the ideas moving through us—**the only way to make this revolution is that we actually *feel* this.**

YOU DON'T CHANGE CULTURE BY GOING VIRAL

I was thinking about William Blake the other day, who was one of the great thinkers of the modern mystical world that birthed modernity. He died in poverty, pretty much unknown, having refused to compromise his vision. William Blake basically says:

- I am not going to go for the popular big podcasts and get 200,000 or 500,000 views.
- I am going to look for the 1,000 people who really *get it*, and they are going to hold it, and they are going to be the 1,000.
- They are going to bring the next 1,000 and the next 1,000, **until my ideas are so embodied in a small group of people at the edge that the edge redefines the center**.

Do you see why this matters?

I want to share with you a book from Princeton University Press, a book that pretty much no one read called *Culture Moves*. How do you make culture moves? My friend Steve sent me the book because it confirmed something I had shared with him in a conversation. He said, *There's this book that no one's read, that says the same thing that you're saying.* I said, *Oh my God, that's fantastic!* Here's what I shared with Steve.

You never change culture by going directly *to the center*.

You don't change culture by starting a popular podcast that gets a billion views, speaking directly into culture, and then everyone simply goes with you.

You don't change culture that way. **You don't change culture by going viral.** *Oh wow, I went viral, that was fantastic. I'm an influencer, I got 3.7 million views*—that's *not* how you change culture.

You change culture by going to the periphery, *to the edge*, to the edges of culture, and creating a *deep radicalism*.

Radical means we go to the root—radical authenticity, radical depth, radical knowing, at the edges of culture. Then the edges of culture become so profound, so shimmering, so alive, so filled with goodness, so filled with truth, and so filled with beauty—and then you create *artifacts*.

That's what William Blake did. William Blake inscribed his knowing into every piece of art, every piece of poetry, and every painting he was commissioned to do. He would just inscribe his vision everywhere.

We often have to create artifacts, so that when you look at them, you're not just *reading* ideas. **The sensemaking then explodes in your body. The sensuality explodes in your body!**

It is very deep, friends. Let's stay in the center of where we are, right here at the edge. It's so deep.

- I go to the edge, and from the edge, I change the center, and then that creates a *Yes!*
- It creates this radical, resounding Yes in the center.

We are at the edge, and that's exactly where we want to be. We want to be creating, at the edge, this deep and profound Great Library—a Great Library of books, of poetry, of embodiment, and of people.

We have to inscribe this on our hearts until we *become* the *dharma*— **we *are* the First Principles and First Value**s. And when you meet someone, you say: *Oh my God, that person is the First Principle and First Value.* They're living it and breathing it, and they can tell the story of it; they can articulate it.

And it's that group of 1,000, and that 500, and that 100, and that 50, and that 10.

From that periphery, we then move into the center—and it explodes.

That's the invitation.

GOD, SACRED TEXT, AND READER OF TEXT ARE ONE

I want to invite everyone, myself and all of us. I want to say it clearly, and I want to use an image from the thirteenth century of a book called *The Zohar*:

- You have to *make love* with the First Principles and First Values.
- You have to let *them* make love to you.
- You have to let the First Principles and First Values, the new Story of Value, love you open—and you also have to love it open.

Then, there's this interaction that happens between your Unique Self— your unique, individuated expression of value, your unique configuration of desire, your unique configuration of intimacy, the Eros that pulses tumescently through you—and the Eros of ideas.

Remember that the ideas come from someone who *felt* something, *validated* that feeling, and then *proved* that feeling was reflecting something true about Reality—and then *wrote it in a book*. A feeling is a pulsing, living organism. When that feeling, that pulsing living organism, meets *you*, meets your own internal pulse—**when those two come together, something explodes into the world.**

That's how it works.

- First there is a Field of Value. It's called Field of Value, but we could call that God, the eternal and evolving *Tao*, the Ground of Value or the Ground of Being itself, the Infinite Intimate, which is our name of God. That's God.
- Then there are the ideas, and let's call that the *dharma*, or the Torah—or, in Bohm's phrase, the Implicate Order, or Ma'at, or Geist, or the Platonic ideas, or the Story of Value embedded in Evolving First Principles and First Values. That's the Torah, that's *the text*.

- Then, there is the reader of the text.

The merger of these three is what evolves the source code of culture.

That is called, in Aramaic—I'm just going to give you one version of it—*Kudsha brich hu yisrael v`orayta chad hu*: **God, sacred text, and reader of text are one**. Wow! *God, Israel, and Torah are one* is the literal translation.

It means that the Field of Value, the text (the specific Story of Value embedded in First Principles and First Values), and the reader all come together.

That's an erotic union. It's a *ménage à trois*. It's the great threesome. **If any of those is missing from the erotic union, if there's only two or only one, there is no erotic union.**

Meaning:

- If you are *not* experiencing yourself as an erotic, living, vibrating expression of the Field of Desire, which is your Unique Self,
- If you're not a unique vibrating, pulsing, exploding configuration of desire and intimacy,
- If you don't understand that *that's* who you are—

—then you can't really read a text. You are just a passive reader, wasting your time listening to a clip.

You have to be Unique Self. **You have to be your unique Eros—*that's the reader*.** Then you have to find and read real texts. We are creating an entirely new Great Library of sacred texts. But go find those texts. Read *Unique Self*. Read *A Return to Eros*. Read other texts. Read William Blake.

The texts we are writing can't be mere fabrications. We're not *making them up*. They're *not* social constructions of Reality.

- We are not making them up, as Yuval Harari claims, parroting the postmodern line—no, they are actually *real*.

- We are not making them up, as Steven Pinker claims, also being trapped in postmodernity.
- We are not making them up, as Shoshana Zuboff claims. She can't quite get this in *Surveillance Capitalism*, so when she critiques the tech plex, her critique falls flat because she refuses to embrace a Field of Value that's real. It's a good initial critique, but she's ends up on the same side as the tech plex—it doesn't work.

We have to be in the *Tao*.

We have to be in the Field of Value.

We have to be immersed in the Field of Value.

We have to be immersed in writing and creating and reading the sacred texts—and reading them as a Unique Self.

We are reading texts as a unique configuration of Eros and desire.

That's the sense that **God, Israel, and Torah are one**.

Another way of saying it is: Buddha, *sangha*, and *dharma*:

- Buddha is the Ground of Being.
- *dharma* is the sacred texts.
- Sangha is the reader in communion with the text.

Wow—is everyone getting that? **This is structural to Cosmos. You cannot create new knowing without this. You cannot understand the Cosmos without that.**

Here's another way to say it, just so you get how structural this is. We can say: *I*, *We*, and *It*.

- *It* is third person. It's the *dharma*, the principles, the Story of Value.
- *We* is me reading, my relationship to the text. I'm the reader

in communion with the text.

- *I* is the God Field, the Buddha Field, the irreducible Unique Self, the unique configuration of Eros that's reading.

Does everyone get that? It's wild, **This is structural to the very source code of Cosmos itself**. In other words, no religion owns *I*, *We*, and *It*.

I, We, and It are the three primordial perspectives that live at the very core of Reality itself.

Kudsha brich hu yisrael v`orayta chad hu in Aramaic:

- God, Israel and Torah.
- The Field of Value, reader, and text.
- Buddha, *sangha*, and *dharma*.
- I, We, and It.

THE CENTER HAS TO BE THE NEW SHARED STORY OF VALUE

Here's what this means. You can't just write the best books in the world— *wow, these books are so great. You're really intelligent, you're really smart...* Like my friend, Sam Harris, who is a really smart guy, but he basically says there is no Field of Value, that it's bullshit, that it doesn't exist. He says that we're making it all up, and it's real *because* we make it up—we are human beings and that's what we've got.

But there is no Field of Value.

There is no place that I surrender, no place that I bow.

However, once there's no Field of Value, you cannot possibly create a shared Story of Value in response to the meta-crisis—because value is not real.

B.F. Skinner said that value is not real. Shoshana Zuboff says value is not real. Steven Pinker says value is not real. The heads of Google and Facebook say value is not real. The MIT Media Lab says value is not real. **If there's no Field of Value, we are going to get to a techno-totalitarian dictatorship, once the human being is reduced to a number.**

So, first, we need a Field of Value.

Second, we need to articulate First Principles and First Values, a Story of Value, study those texts that are telling that story, and immerse ourselves in them.

- If there is no sacred text, you are basically jumping from book to book, from video to video, from podcast to podcast.
- If you don't have a central set of shared texts that create a community, you're done. You can't do it. **You have to have a central set of shared texts that are at the center.**

I want you to get something deep here—there's tears in my eyes.

I believe in teachers and I believe in teaching, and I'm obviously staking my life on teachers teaching. That's what I do. *But the teacher can never be the center.* **The center has to be the shared Story of Value itself, the First Principles and First Values themselves.** If it is only based on a charismatic teacher, it will always crash and fail.

That's what we mean by the democratization of enlightenment. It's what we mean by the democratization of sensemaking. We need a set of shared texts that operate in a shared set of First Principles and First Values, at the very center.

I'll just give you an example.

I was sitting with my friend, the Dalai Lama, who invited me to come visit him after we had a fight that I've told you guys about before. And I gave him my skullcap, my Hebraic *yarmulke*, which I wore ritually. I gave it to him to wear for a day, and he did. We were at a conference, at the Pope's summer residence. At the end of the day, he was kind of impish, with a twinkle in his eye. He put my yarmulke in his pocket, and he said, *Hey*

Marc, if you want your yarmulke back, come visit me in Dharamsala (that's not exactly how it happened, there's other pieces to the story, but that's enough for now).

So, I go to Dharamsala to get my yarmulke back, and we have a wonderful conversation. We had a great time together, and he asked me, *How did the Hebrew wisdom tradition survive?* I said there are two principles that allowed this Hebrew wisdom to survive:

- One is, we are not based on the Dalai Lama. It's an audacious thing to say, but it's true. We're not based on a Dalai Lama. It's a very big deal. It's not based on a Dalai Lama. It's not based on a God teacher.
- Two, it's based on a set of living, evolving sacred texts, rooted in First Principles and First Values, that *everybody* studies— not just the scholars, not just the elite, not just the intellectuals. Everyone sits and studies and absorbs and comments. **It's not based on a God teacher, but a living, evolving set of sacred texts.**

What's at the center of One Mountain, Many Paths, and the center of our Center for World Philosophy and Religion? I'll tell you what the center is *not*:

It's not Barbara Marx Hubbard. It's not Marc Gafni. The center is the *dharma*, the First Principles, the values themselves.

And they are so strong because **they are studied by an entire community who are living these First Principles and First Values, and who begin to embody them**. Then everyone in the community brings their Unique Self to the story.

I want to be quite rigorous here for a second, and I know everyone's about to get mad at me. So could everyone just prepare to get mad at me? That way when you get mad, you won't be surprised. Get ready to get mad, here we go.

When someone raises their hand and says, *Well, I disagree*, I say: *Really? You disagree? Why?*

Well, because it doesn't feel right.

Then I ask, *Have you studied the text carefully? What do you mean, you disagree? Don't tell me you disagree—tell me why. Step inside, know the text. Master them the best way you can. And if you've stepped inside, and you've mastered them, I want to hear what you have to say. If you don't, then shut up.*

I want you to get this, because what happens is, people often raise their hand and they say, *Oh, I disagree*. Don't do that. Instead: **Become a master.** You don't go to a physics class and just raise your hand and say: *Hey, Mr. Einstein, that doesn't feel right to me what you're saying. It really bothers me, it awakens an early traumatic reaction in me, and I feel really unsafe around what you're saying, Mr. Einstein.*

No. Study physics first, and *then* challenge Einstein, and then knock Einstein off and take his place, which is indeed what people are doing in quantum physics.

In other words, **step into the** *dharma* **the same way you step into a karate dojo. Become a master.**

And if I'm the sensei in this dojo, unseat me. Write new chapters, add to it, change it—but *from within*, because you've mastered the principles, because you can feel them, because you know them, because they are alive in you. Only then challenge it, deepen it, and add it from within.

The only true master is one who teaches the student with the intent of the student becoming a master.

And the only way this can be true is if both the student and master bow to the larger Field of Value. Does everyone get that? **Both the student and master bow to the larger Field of Value.** And *then* if the student comes and says something, beautiful.

I'm going to give you an example, just to make this real. My dear friend Zachary Stein—who actually lives with me in the Center house, where he's the Co-President of the Center—started studying with me as a student, and we have a teacher-student relationship to this day. But we also have a *beloved* relationship, and we also have a *partner* relationship, and we also have a *colleague* relationship. Zak *stepped in*, and the most important thing is that he gets to grow and to deepen both by remaining a student and becoming a master himself in his own fields.

Absorb the *dharma*, **absorb every word of it, become it—then add to it.** I call it *Zak-ify*. But he first had to actually *master* it, *know* it, know his own fields of mastery, and *then* add a dimension to it through the prisms of education and development that are new and unique to the *dharma*.

In other words:

- Yes, there *is* a teacher-student relationship—and *then* step in, blow it away, and become a master.
- Then raise up your own students, and they raise up their own students.

We need to be both teachers and students. But we need teachers and students where the main job of the students is to become a master.

My greatest joy is when someone gets something in the *dharma* that I didn't see. *Wow, I didn't see that.* But not because they just *claimed it*—because **they stepped in so deeply that they saw and felt something through their Unique Self that's not available to me.** And then when they share it with me, oh my God, I bow! I bow at their feet.

That's what we mean by Unique Self.

YOU HAVE TO KNOW HOW TO BE A STUDENT

To the precise extent that you're *not* in your own purity, that you're *not* in your own sincerity, that you're in an *ego* game, you are playing a lazy game, running from podcast to podcast and saying the words, but you're not *deep in*. You don't actually *step in*.

When you step in, you have to learn how to be a student. There's nothing I love more than being a student myself.

I'll share with you guys that I'm reading a book that is almost impossible to read. It was written by my teacher with whom I haven't talked in over forty years—a classical Orthodox Jewish master who disagrees with everything I'm doing now. He wrote a doctorate at Harvard when he was 19, called *Henry Moore: The Rational Theology of a Cambridge Platonist*. It's almost impossible to read, and I am reading this book now.

You can't even get it anymore, but I found it, and I'm reading it cover-to-cover, word-for-word, because I want to absorb the words of my master, my teacher, even though he completely disagrees with me. He thinks I've become a heretic, that I've stepped away from Orthodox Judaism in a way that's wrong, and that this whole thing we are doing is wrong.

It doesn't matter. He's my teacher, so I want to absorb every word he says. I dream about him two or three times a week. Oh my God!

You first have to know how to be a student, to receive, to get quiet enough that you open yourself up—and then you can step in.

For most of us, our relationship to the *dharma* is not going to be like my relationship to Orthodox Judaism. I had to leave that world in order to create the world we want to create. Here, we can create together. But step in with your mastery.

If I can beg you for anything, I beg you for your own mastery.

Become a master. Step in.

That's what we mean when we say Unique Self Symphony,

Unique Self Symphony is not just, *Oh, we're all hanging out and working together.* That's one expression of Unique Self Symphony, when we're all doing what we do to make this work. That's one beautiful, holy expression of Unique Self Symphony. That's one gorgeous expression of Unique Self Symphony, where we are all holding a different piece, and we all have different roles. That's beautiful.

But there's another level of Unique Self Symphony, where we step in and become, each of us, masters in a particular way.

That's my dream. My dream is to be surrounded by people who have become masters. Because any teacher that doesn't want their students to become masters is a tyrant. Don't listen to them. Just walk away.

But to become a master, you've got to come in with your Unique Self. You've got to come in and move beyond the trauma and the ego, and find your purity.

Oh my God, be sensual. Know! Be carnal, be alive. Engage the text, study.

WHO WE ARE AS UNIQUE SELF SYMPHONY

You don't have to study *everything*. If I can just offer a little piece of just tender advice: **pick one field, something you're interested in.**

- Let's say you're reading *A Return to Eros*, where we talk about the twelve faces of Eros. So pick one face: being on the inside, giving and receiving are one, whatever. Pick one of the twelve faces, and become the master of that face.
- Let's say you're in the Unique Self teaching. Pick one chapter in the *Unique Self* book, and become the master of that.

In other words, pick one set of ideas and say: Wow, I just listened to that One Mountain, there was this set of ideas, I'm going to go deeper into that, or I'm going to become the master of this, whatever it is. **To step into mastery *is* what it means to become Unique Self Symphony.**

That's what it means to democratize enlightenment.

And notice:

- We are not saying that there are no sacred texts. There *are* sacred texts.
- We are not saying there is no Field of Value. There *is* a Field of Value, and the Field of Value is what we call the Divine. And there's a set of sacred texts that we're writing together.
- And then there are the individual, Unique Self, erotic masters of the text.

I first become a student. I never graduate from being a student. But at the same time, I also become a master.

I try my best to operate as a master and a student all the time. So here I am, I just bought this book a few days ago, and I'm just in devotion late at night, literally *absorbing* the words of my teacher—in complete devotion and complete surrender, as I open up to absorb, to receive. **That power is the power of Unique Self Symphony**.

WE HAVE TO LISTEN TO *SHE*

We are going to end with prayer.

There are all sorts of people, beautiful people, who say: *Marc, don't do the prayer thing, it's too religious.* Let's do the prayer thing—but we are not going to pray entirely like the old religions do.

- We're not praying to a cosmic vending-machine God, where you put in a quarter and get a result.

- ◆ We're praying to the Infinite Intimate—that's the new name of God. God who is the Infinity of Intimacy, who both holds us and lives in us at the same time, holding that paradox.
- ◆ We bring before the Infinite Intimate, before Her altar, all of our brokenness and all of our wholeness—*our holy and our broken Hallelujah.*

And we offer up our prayer.

We pray for our friends, and for our uncles, and for our sons, and for our mothers, and for our daughters. And then we pray for our people.

Then we pray for the whole world, for every human being, and we pray for every animal, and we pray for the biosphere.

Then we pray for our place as Earth in the larger galactic field, which is disclosing itself. We're not just an Earth field but part of a larger galactic field.

And we pray for all the incarnations.

And in these prayers, we are asking, we are demanding, we are begging, we are affirming, but we're not only asking. **When we speak the truths of our prayer, the yearnings of our prayer, they are inscribed in the Akashic field.** They're inscribed in the Field of Value—and something moves and something shifts. So we ask for everything. We turn to the Infinite Intimate that both lives in us and holds us, and we ask for everything.

And so as we go into this prayer, Leonard Cohen has been very, very beautiful, and he's going to sing it for us, and we're going to step in. And as he sings in One Mountain, I'm going to ask everyone just to write your prayers. Oh my God, thank you, thank you, thank you, thank you, thank you, thank you, thank you!

I planned to talk about something completely different today. It was not my intention to talk about this at all. I wanted to actually go into the ten laws today. But we have to listen to *She*, and *She* took over.

She just whispered and said, *no, we have to talk about this.*

We have to actually get this.

We have to get who we are.

We have to get the democratization of greatness.

We have to get this *I*, *We*, and *It*: this Buddha, sangha, and *dharma*.

This is the democratization of enlightenment, a new way of being together and being in community, and just to blow this away.

Oh my God, take us inside.

Holy and broken Hallelujah, it doesn't matter which you heard.

CHAPTER ELEVEN

THE TRANSFORMATIONAL YOGA OF WRITING OUTRAGEOUS LOVE LETTERS: AWAKENING AS HOMO AMOR, THE NEW HUMAN AND THE NEW HUMANITY

Episode 336 — March 19, 2023

YOUR LIFE IS AN OUTRAGEOUS LOVE STORY

Over the last few weeks, we've been telling one chapter in the story of Outrageous Love.

We did a week on Outrageous Love:

- What is Outrageous Love? Why the term *Outrageous Love*?
- What does an Outrageous Lover do? Commit Outrageous Acts of Love. The divine Outrageous Act of Love, the great manifestation of Reality, is where the Infinite Intimate turns and says *I need you* to Reality. We commit our Outrageous Acts of Love because that's what an Outrageous Lover does.
- We know which Outrageous Acts of Love we commit: those that are a function of our Unique Self and our unique set of allurements, those which Reality desperately needs from us. We must take our Unique Risk to commit our Outrageous Acts of Love.

149

What we are going to talk about today is: **where do we get the energy to do this?**

- ◆ Do we meditate? It's always a good idea.
- ◆ Do we pray? Yes, that's also always a good idea.

But there's *a new yoga*, and we're going to talk today about the new yoga that is the fuel of this revolution.

EVOLUTIONARY LOVE CODE: YOUR LIFE IS AN OUTRAGEOUS LOVE LETTER

Based on the leading edges of interior and exterior science, the most accurate statement of human identity is: human beings are, to a person, unique incarnations of Outrageous Love, which itself is not a mere social construction, but the heart of existence itself.

To say it simply, you are an Outrageous Lover.

What do Outrageous Lovers do? Outrageous Lovers commit Outrageous Acts of Love.

The Outrageous Love needed to commit Outrageous Acts of Love is activated through the practice of writing Outrageous Love Letters.

Your Unique Self is God's Outrageous Love Letter to you, as you.

Your Outrageous Acts of Love are your Outrageous Love Letters back to God.

The way to awaken as an Outrageous Lover is the practice of writing Outrageous Love Letters, and the ultimate awakening of the Outrageous Lover is the realization that **your life itself is an Outrageous Love Letter.**

How do you awaken the energy of Outrageous Love—which is, remember, not ordinary love, not a social construction, but *the heart of existence itself*? How do you awaken that? How do you access that?

Part of the structure of Reality is that we have to *step inside*:

- ♦ We have to activate a yoga in order to access a *dharma*,
- ♦ No gnosis, no real knowing, is ever attained without transformative practice.

That's critical, whether that's in the classical, exterior sciences or in the interior sciences. **Without a rigorous, transformative practice, we don't attain gnosis.** Without transforming and transfiguring something in myself, I never have actual knowledge.

I cannot get knowledge only by moving around in my brain and my mind.

I cannot only stay in the realm of words.

I have to engage in profound yoga in order to access *dharma*. I need to engage in *First Practices* in order to access First Principles and First Values.

A core practice that we have introduced in our community of Outrageous Lovers, in this One Mountain, Many Paths, is the practice of writing Outrageous Love Letters.

Evolution becomes conscious to itself through our awakening to the realization that my life, your life, each of our lives, is an Outrageous Love Letter.

What you realize is that you're the messenger that forgot your message— but the message is you, encrypted as your Unique Self. **You awaken by remembering that you are the personal face of the evolutionary impulse, and by remembering this through your own unique personal evolution of consciousness, you participate in the evolution of love.**

Let's go deep. Who knows if we even have another week or two weeks? Let's go deep, this is a forever moment.

To awaken as an Outrageous Lover is to become intimate with Reality itself. You recognize that you are living in an Intimate Universe, in which you are seen, witnessed, addressed, and called. You are called to realize that existence needs you as an intimate partner, that Reality needs your service, and that your Outrageous Acts of Love become the text of the Outrageous Love Letter, which is your life.

Your life is an Outrageous Love Letter, and the text of your life is an Outrageous Act of Love.

And then you ask, *What is my life?*

My life is an Outrageous Love Story.

Living life as an Outrageous Love Letter comes from the realization that my life is an Outrageous Love Story, that it's chapter and verse in The Universe: A Love Story. And the Outrageous Acts of Love that I commit, which are a function of my Unique Self, for which I'm willing to take my Unique Risk—that's my Outrageous Love Story.

When I awaken as the evolutionary impulse, I activate my capacity to commit Outrageous Act of Love. When that happens, I become intimate with self and intimate with the universe, and the universe comes into intimate communion with you, with me.

LOVE YOUR WAY TO ENLIGHTENMENT

The practice that activates the truth that my life is an Outrageous Love Letter is the practice of writing Outrageous Love Letters. We need the capacity to not only wait until we feel it, but to *cause* the feeling, to go on the journey, to *choose*—so you can access Outrageous Love even when you're not spontaneously feeling it.

The practice and the yoga of writing Outrageous Love Letters kindles Outrageous Love.

The practice emerges originally from *the Song of Songs* of Solomon, in the great canon of Hebrew wisdom, which is the great canon of Western civilization, which plays in Islam and in Christianity and in the native traditions. *The Song of Solomon*, **which is considered the most sacred book of the ancient canon, is essentially a series of Outrageous Love notes between a lover and a beloved.**

That one sentence is a big deal. That's not a given. It's not the way that the public exoteric tradition understands it—but if you know how to read more deeply, it's a set of Outrageous Love notes between a lover and a beloved.

The Song of Solomon, which is called the Holy of Holies—the deepest of the deep, *lifnai v'lifnim*. To be *lifnai v'lifnim* is to be on the Inside of the Inside, in the deepest face of the deepest face. I have to write Outrageous Love Letters.

Over the last decade, we've written thousands of Outrageous Love Letters:

- ◆ You can write an Outrageous Love Letter to yourself.
- ◆ You can write an Outrageous Love Letter to a split-off part of yourself that you want to become intimate with.
- ◆ You can write an Outrageous Love Letter to a future dream that you want to live.
- ◆ You can write one to another person, to someone in your circle, to a romantic beloved, to a beloved friend, or someone you're working with.
- ◆ You can write one to someone who shows up and you meet online. You write each other Outrageous Love Letters because you recognize your beauty in each other's comments, and you get together offline, and you say: *Oh my God, let's be Outrageous Lovers.*

153

That doesn't mean we're going to have sex. Outrageous Love is not about sex. It doesn't mean we are going to get a U-haul and move in together. It means we're going to see each other fully, open our hearts, allow ourselves to fall in love, and love madly—because our love lists are too short.

The key instruction for writing an Outrageous Love Letter is you exaggerate until you are accurate. You describe the other person in ways that you're never allowed to, until you actually get to the full accurate beauty of who you're writing Outrageous Love Letters to. You might think that to love outrageously is beyond your capacity, that only saints or enlightened beings love outrageously. Not true. It's time for what we've called, over the last fifteen years, *the democratization of enlightenment.*

The democratization of enlightenment is the democratization of Outrageous Love.

This means we're not going to meditate our way to enlightenment, and we're not going to pray our way to enlightenment—**we're going to *love* our way to enlightenment**. To do that, we've got to democratize Outrageous Love.

YOU ARE RUMI AND YOUR IMAGINATION IS A FIGMENT OF GOD

There is no prophet to wait for. Rumi is not going to write your letter for you. Pasternak is not going to write your letter for you. Shakespeare is not going to write your letter for you.

You are going to write it.

You are Outrageous Love.

The future is you. The old top-down world of religion and governance is over. The old command-and-control is over.

154

There's no Messiah that's coming. *She's* already come, and *She's* you.

- These aren't words of love parading in pretty costumes.
- This is the deepest truth of Cosmos.
- This is not a casual activity we do every week. This is the deepest truth of Reality.
- This is the First Principle and First Value of Eros, the realization that emerges from the deepest consideration of Reality that we can do today, based on both the interior and exterior sciences.

The practice is simple. All you need is your imagination. But you do have to imagine. **God may be a figment of your imagination, that may be true. But your imagination is a figment of God**. When you write Outrageous Love Letters, you let your imagination, your fantasy, soar—and you fantasize of a world of depth, a world of goodness, and a world of truth.

We actually begin to become utopia.

One of the things we first do is actually envision the dystopian possibility— it's hard to imagine, but it's real. But we are not only about invoking dystopia. **In order to respond to dystopia, we have to begin to live utopia.**

- We have to embody the alternative.
- We have to be able to live the dream of what's possible.
- We have to begin to live and be *Homo amor*.
- We have to begin to live utopia.

The practice that awakens *Homo amor*, that awakens your deeper identity as an Outrageous Love Letter, is no less and no more than writing Outrageous Love Letters yourself.

We usually rely on the great poets or sages for words of love. We want to send someone words of love, we find some quote from some master that's written in a card, and we send it to someone. Often, people use Rumi, the great Persian poet, and you send someone a love letter with a quote from

Rumi. But why would you send someone a love letter with a quote from a dead Persian? No, you are Outrageous Love. We have to democratize Outrageous Love. *You* are Rumi.

It's your Outrageous Love Letter that will blow open Reality.

We have to *learn* this practice.

- ◆ The first turning of the wheel was meditation.
- ◆ The second turning of the wheel, prayer.
- ◆ The third turning of the wheel, as we invoke *Homo amor*, is we learn the practice of writing Outrageous Love Letters, to those you are close to and those you may not know so well but who are part of your life.

And when you're ready, you can even write an Outrageous Love Letter to people you feel are adversaries or competitors. **This practice liberates the unique flame of Outrageous Love that is the currency of your very existence, and it awakens your capacity to commit Outrageous Acts of Love.** Wow!

YOU ARE THE OUTRAGEOUS LOVE LETTER FROM THE INFINITY OF INTIMACY

Outrageous Love Letters make us ready to play the most outrageous game possible, in which Outrageous Love becomes conscious through you. **Reality has an appetite for value, and Reality's highest value is that we become Outrageous Lovers.** Reality's highest value is that Outrageous Love awakens at the human level.

At the human level:

- ◆ We become conscious of our identity as Outrageous Love.
- ◆ We become conscious of our identity as *unique configurations* of Outrageous Love.
- ◆ We commit Outrageous Acts of Love.

When we commit Outrageous Acts of Love, we are God's hands, and Goddess's hands, and Goddess's verbs, and Goddess's nouns, and Goddess's dangling modifiers. We are unique configurations of intimacy.

Remember, God is the Infinite Intimate—that's the name of God that we've invoked. God is the Infinity of Intimacy, so when we become Outrageous Acts of Love, when we are divine hands, and we participate in the Field of Goddess, we're on the inside of Goddess's face. To be on the inside of Goddess's face is to live on the inside.

When I live on the inside, I realize I'm participating in the Field of Goddess, and **my sacred autobiography becomes a love letter back to God**. In other words:

- ◆ God/Goddess writes us a love letter, which is our Unique Self.
- ◆ Then we write an Outrageous Love Letter, back to God which is our Outrageous Act of Love.

Feel this with me; there's just one last step. This is the Inside of the Inside of the interior sciences. We are expressing it in a new language, but this is core to Reality. This is a gnosis that you can only know through practicing deeply—because remember, all gnosis, all real knowing comes from trans-formative practice. Here it is:

All of Reality is an Outrageous Love Letter from Goddess to you, from the universe to you.

Remember—the god you don't believe in doesn't exist, so you can read God as the Tao, the Reality Principle, the Implicate Order, the evolutionary impulse, the Infinite Intimate. God's Outrageous Love Letter to you is not a simple form letter—it's a personal love letter addressed to you. **That love letter is your radical irreducible uniqueness. Your radical irreducible uniqueness is Reality's personal Outrageous Love Letter to you.**

It took the evolutionary impulse, scientifically speaking, some 13.7 billion years of synergy to write your personal love letter. Its content, texture, and tone are utterly unique, written and intended only for you. This is the Outrageous Love Letter written from Infinity to you, written in the script of your Unique Self.

Once you awaken and live your Unique Self expression, taking your Unique Risk and committing your Outrageous Acts of Love as an awakened Outrageous Lover, then you're writing an Outrageous Love Letter back to Goddess.

Imagine Goddess, friends, the evolutionary impulse, sending an Outrageous Love Letter to you in the form of your atomic, cellular, and interior spiritual signature. Feel Her, feel Goddess yearning over the millennia, as She waits for Her letter to you to be delivered over billions of years. And then you're born. She's intending you, choosing you, recognizing you, love-desiring you, and adoring you. But she's also needing you.

When you're born, the clock starts ticking, and She waits with bated breath, desperately yearning to receive your return letter to Her.

Imagine Her going to the mailbox every day, and opening it up to see, *did the letter come yet?*

That's the letter that you write back to Goddess. That's your Unique Self, committing your Outrageous Acts of Love.

In other words, when you awaken to your Unique Self:

- You're awakening as an irreducibly unique expression of the zero-point field, the God Field, the Field of Outrageous LoveIntelligence.
- You're awakening into your divinity.
- You're on the inside of God's face.

That's when you become an *imaginal cell* of new humanity—and **your life story, your Outrageous Love Story, and your Outrageous Acts of Love**

are the Outrageous Love Letter from God to God, signed with your name. So in fact, because you *are* Goddess, Goddess is writing *Herself* a return letter, and that return letter is signed with the signature of your life.

This is the realization that changes everything.

You begin to be lived as Outrageous Love.

You begin to live the Outrageous Love that you imagined in the dreams you forgot about so long ago.

You begin to commit Outrageous Acts of Love.

Outrageous Love gives you direct and sustained access to a level of aliveness, wisdom, Eros, and joy that not only have we forgotten— but we forgot that we've forgotten.

Outrageous Love is the memory of our future, of the new human and new humanity.

We are going to have a place where we can write and share our Outrageous Love Letters, talk about what Outrageous Acts of Love we've committed, and inspire each other. We are just beginning. Today, I wanted to take the next step, with your permission, tenderly, gently, to begin to unpack this.

What does it mean to be alive? **My life is an Outrageous Love Letter back to Goddess.** She wrote me an Outrageous Love Letter, my Unique Self. When I awaken to my Unique Self, when I commit Outrageous Acts of Love, I'm writing that letter back to Her that She is desperately yearning for, and that I'm desperately yearning to write.

This gives me the ultimate aliveness and joy, in the midst of all the agony and the ecstasy.

CHAPTER TWELVE

WHAT'S MISSING FROM CULTURE: A MODEL OF SELF—ANSWERING THE QUESTION, "WHO AM I?"

Episode 375 — December 17, 2023

WE NEED TO DEEPEN OUR UNDERSTANDING OF REALITY

In order to emerge, in order to transmute, in order to transfigure—in order to actually do what I'm born to do, which is to become fully human, a process of profound and kind of gorgeous transformation—I have to be able to deepen my understanding of Reality.

I have to deepen my knowing.

I have to deepen my ability to access deep currents of wisdom.

Particularly in this moment of abject confusion in the world, I need to be deep in the *dharma*, in a systemic vision that allows me to understand Reality as deeply as I can—and then, from that place, to hold the mystery.

To be in the *dharma*, I have to *study*. I can't just consume information in this strange postmodern way, where the postmodern mind says:

- There is no storyline.
- There is no essential, inherent connectivity.
- There is no inherent *telos*.
- There is no plotline.
- It's not going anywhere.

The postmodern mind's exterior expression is the internet—where you're reading, and then there's a link, and you jump to something else. Then there's another link, your attention is hijacked, and it goes someplace else. Then you do a little doom scrolling, you move all over the place, and two hours have gone by.

Everyone recognizes this experience. The internet is structured and built to do this. **The structure of the internet is the exterior manifestation of the interior experience of the postmodern mind**—as opposed to the deep experience of reading:

- Where I'm following a plotline.
- Where I'm on the Inside of the Inside.
- Where I'm able to feel Reality, map Reality, find my place in it, sense its fragrance and its plotline, and its direction, its Eros, its *telos*.

Instead I'm jumping around, tugged at, pulled to and fro. The aftertaste is disorientation and confusion.

The structure of the internet is the exterior expression of postmodernity's deconstruction of a Field of Value. The Field of Value is a narrative with a plotline—it's going somewhere, and this invites the human being to *aspire*:

- I'm reaching for something.
- I realize that I'm part of the Field of Evolution, and I want to transform.

And I realize that my transformation is *real*.

My transformation is the aspirational architecture of the Cosmos.

When I don't aspire, when there is no aspiration, then there is no plotline to Cosmos. **If there is no *aspire*, then there is only *conspire*, which leads to conspiracy theory.**

Since I don't see the plotline, and it *cannot be* that there is no plotline—something must be organizing this, something must be guiding the action because you can *sense* that there must be a storyline, you have the sense of storyline deep in your first-person experience—we go to conspiracy theory, and we *fabricate* plotlines.

Not *all* conspiracy theories are entirely fabricated plotlines. Some conspiracy theories have truth to them, and they're labeled conspiracy theories in order to deflect from their truth.

But there is also a large body of conspiracy theories that jump from this fact point to that fact point to the next fact point, all of which are independently valid, but we don't know how to put them all together. There's a sense that there must be a coherent plotline, but we can't find one, so it manifests conspiracy theory.

HOW TO STUDY DHARMA

We come together in One Mountain, Many Paths, in this time between worlds and time between stories, and we are committed to evolving the source code. We ultimately know that the only effective way to respond to the meta-crisis is to tell a new Story of Value—a new superstructure of Reality that naturally raises all boats and allows us to see new possibilities of infrastructure and social structure: the way we do technology, the way we do politics.

A new Story of Value, this evolution of the cultural source code, completely redefines economics, redefines technology, redefines politics, and raises all boats. We make this da Vinci move just like they did in the Renaissance—in that previous time between worlds and time between stories.

With respect and honor and love and delight, I am suggesting that **you have to develop a way to study**. One of the ways that I study is:

- Step one: I listen deeply. I take it all in. I recapitulate it. I review it. I *swallow* it, so that it's part of me, I know it. It's not only knowledge in my mind. It's not only knowledge in my heart. Like the Rastas say, *it's in my bones*. Or as the Hasidic masters say, *it's in my toenails*. It's the knowing that I have in my toenails. It's in me.

- Step two: Once I've swallowed it all, once it's in me, then I can add to it. I can step out, look at it, and I can say, *Oh, let me add something to that. Let me clarify that. Let me challenge this in order to make this more clear.*

It's such a beautiful paradox.

On the one hand, I'm fully open to receive. When some people listen, they're listening for what's wrong. They're actually *not* listening. They're not letting it in. They find what they think is a chink in the armor, and **they lose the capacity to listen with mad love**—and that's what we have to do in relationship.

When I listen in relationship, I have to listen with mad love, take it all in, absorb it—and then from that place, okay, now maybe we can evolve it.

This way of listening to *dharma* is not an abandonment of self.

- I'm listening from my deepest self. I take it in. It actually reconfigures and reformulates my self. That's level one. We would call that *surrender*—full submission. I receive and swallow the *dharma*.

- Then step two would be, I step back. I rewrite it with the same sentences, but maybe I've changed the order. That's the recapitulation. Or I review it carefully. I've stepped out and I look at it really deeply. That's level two. That's called *havdalah*. I separate from it, I look at it, and I reorganize it. I operate on it.
- Only then you can do level three. Level three is called *sweetness*. It means I can add something new. My voice adds something to the symphony that wasn't there before.

I can begin to contribute originally, but only if I do step one and step two. It's critical. Without that, I can't become a master. I can't become a person who knows how to do sensemaking.

It means I can't become the new human. I can't speak my voice into the Unique Self Symphony.

DECONSTRUCTION OF VALUE LEADS TO THE DECONSTRUCTION OF FACTS

What's our intention here? **We want to evolve the source code of consciousness and culture in response to the meta-crisis in this time between worlds and time between stories.**

I talked to my daughter this morning in Israel. She is deeply enmeshed in the fabric of Israeli society. She is devastatingly good and devastatingly brilliant. And I said to her that I'm blown away by her unbearable grace—in life, as a parent, and also as a figure in public life over the last several months.

My daughter is eminently practical. She speaks with a matter-of-fact yet deep ethos, like, "This is what needs to be done. This is what's happening." She doesn't talk about things like the Field of Value. And then I realized that the ability to have a conversation—about Israel, about Gaza, about anything—requires both fact *and* value. **Fact itself is a value: the notion**

that you have to have the facts before you can say anything about something is itself a value.

Premodern reality was all about values, and every religion said *we* own the values, and *we* have the direct revelation. Facts don't really matter.

If science was in the way of the value of the church, it was put aside. If discoveries in researching the human body contradicted the dogma of Galen's medicine—which was the church dogma of medicine—then science was put aside.

It was all about value. Facts didn't matter.

Along comes modernity, which says, *Value is made up, only facts matter.* David Hume: *You guys made up value. What matters is facts.* And everyone thought, *Okay, now we'll be able—through facts—to create science, and we'll create a shared narrative of progress.*

Along comes postmodernity, which at its very core says, *Facts don't matter because a fact is a value, and values aren't real.* Postmodernity says, *Not only are values contrived, but facts themselves are a value. The notion that facts matter is a value, and values have been deconstructed, so facts don't matter anymore.* **What's left is the story that you make up.**

If all that's left is the story that you're making up, and your story becomes your identity, then:

- You cannot create peace.
- You cannot create coherence.
- You cannot create intimacy.
- You cannot create a world that works for everyone.
- You cannot create justice.

You create only a world of radical polarization and unimaginable suffering—what we see in so many parts of the world today.

All of that together—this deconstruction of value, which created a deconstruction of fact, which led to everybody lost in their own individual sto-

165

ry without any ability to see the whole and create a shared story for the whole—generates the meta-crisis. The meta-crisis is the explosion of the planetary boundaries, which undermine the substrate we need to survive, based on individual interests. Country against country, company against company, person against person—rivalrous conflict governed by win/lose metrics drives the meta-crisis.

This inability to create a coherent narrative will inexorably lead either directly to the very death of humanity or to the death of *our* humanity— to the creation of a totalitarian state based on restoring order, aided by some version of artificial general intelligence, which in a short period of time will lock in its value structure and apply it to the whole system.

That's where we're going.

WE NEED A NEW STORY OF VALUE ROOTED IN BOTH VALUE AND FACT

The response to that has to be a revolution of a Copernican nature.

---

*We have to completely re-vision
how we vision.*

The beginning of it is knowing that there actually *is* a Field of Value, that value is actually *real*.

We reclaim value, which was rejected by modernity and postmodernity.

- ◆ We accept all the reasons that modernity rejected value.
- ◆ We understand the problem.
- ◆ We solve those problems.
- ◆ We create a new vision of value.

That's what we're doing here at the Center. And the first book on that is coming in about two weeks, called *First Principles & First Values*.

We live in the Field of Value—and from that deep realization, we can tell this new Story of Value. This new Story of Value becomes a global story, a global narrative, a shared story. **This story is based on both value and fact together.** We begin to have a world narrative that doesn't erase diversity, but is a context for diversity.

It's a world story of value as a context for diversity. We can finally have a conversation.

For example, Richard Nixon and John Kennedy were on opposite sides of the political aisle, but were really good friends because they had a shared story of value that they both participated in.

We need a shared Story of Value rooted both in fact and value that every human being on the planet—from China, to Russia, to Afghanistan, to Israel, to the United States, to South America—can participate in. *Everyone has a seat at the table.*

It's vital that we can empirically *validate* that story. It aligns with our understanding of interiors and exteriors, based on the deepest possible human research that we can do.

And that story evolves. It's an evolving story of value. **It's the new *Tao*—an eternal *Tao* that is also an evolving *Tao*.**

That's our context.

You might think, "Okay, I got that already. I've heard all that before."

But something shifts when you begin to actually swallow and integrate it. When I'm saying it again, I'm not saying it again *at* you. I'm not giving a talk *to you*—I am reorienting it in my own heart, mind, and body. Just so you know, I do this multiple times during the day and night because that's how I ground myself. I know that there are some people, even some of the people who are my closest students and friends, who think "All right, we've heard him talk about that." They tune out. "Let's wait for the new thing."

That's a mistake! Don't do that.

Every time we recapitulate it, we're doing something new. We are deepening. And it's always new.

I've had the privilege, along with *She*, of originating a lot of this *dharma*, and I still recapitulate it for myself all the time because this is not *a talk*. This is not information on a podcast. **We are practicing by locating ourselves and articulating this new Story of Value.**

To fully locate ourselves, we need to know the answer to the question of *Who I am*.

There are two basic ways into that question, two models of self. One we call the Four Selves, and the other we call the Three Selves.

FOUR SELVES MODEL

What's the Four Selves model? I'm going to assume that everyone knows this, but I want to touch it briefly and add something exciting to it.

Four Selves means that when I ask, *Who are you?* you can answer in four ways.

SEPARATE SELF AND THE WESTERN ENLIGHTENMENT: I AM A PUZZLE PIECE

One way is the classic answer given by Western society: I am a *separate self*.

I'm a good individual citizen of the world.

The boundaries of me are my skin. I am my skin-encapsulated ego. That's the end of myself.

I can see things, I can know things, but basically I'm a separate self.

The way we often talk about that is: I am a puzzle piece.

There might not even be a puzzle. I'm just an individual puzzle piece. There might be part of me that yearns for the larger puzzle, but that's just an illusion. That's a delusion. I'm a separate self. That's what I am. That's how the West understands who I am. It's called an *ego* self.

To be a healthy ego self, a healthy separate self, is the main job of Western psychology. I go back to my early childhood, and I see where I was traumatized, and I try and work out my relationship to my mother, and to my caretakers, and to my culture. I am trying to work out the appropriate flow of energy within my separate self.

That's the basic answer to the question of self.

That's the Western understanding of *enlightenment*. The Western Enlightenment said, "Who are you? You're a separate self." And it's not all bad, this view: all the dignity, all the goodness, all the truth, and all the beauty of modernity come from this realization.

The premodern idea that I am part of some larger people is absurd, according to this perspective. That's a violation. That's what causes suffering. The notion that I'm part of this larger whatever is nonsense. I am a separate self. I am not intrinsically part of any country, any people. I am a separate self.

That notion of identity was a momentous leap forward in many ways. It created the notion of modern human rights. All human rights are based on this realization: I'm a separate self, and I have distinct boundaries, and I have rights. These are universal human rights. Fantastic.

That's the separate self.

TRUE SELF AND MYSTICAL ENLIGHTENMENT: I AM THE PUZZLE

Eastern enlightenment said, *No, no, no. There is another level of self. Separate self is not actually who you are. That's a mistake.* Not just Eastern enlightenment, but mystical enlightenment across traditions, which said, *That's not who you are. That's a mistake. That's an illusion.* **Who you really are is inseparable from the field.**

169

What's the field? In classical Buddhism, let's say Theravada Buddhism, it's the Field of *Awareness*, **True Self**. I am inseparable from the Field of Awareness. **Who I really am is not the story of my separate self.**

The boundary of the separate self is an illusion. And that boundary *itself*—which the Western Enlightenment says *ends* suffering—is, according to Eastern enlightenment traditions, *the source* of all suffering. You only move beyond suffering if you realize that your true nature, your True Self, is one with the Field of Awareness.

Now let me add to that. Over the last fifteen years, I've tried to challenge that notion of True Self. The True Self means not just that you're one with the Field of Awareness or Consciousness, but **you are also one with the Field of Desire**. **You are one with the Field of Eros.**

The experience of True Self is of being interconnected and inextricably connected with the entire field. You can *feel* the whole field, and the whole field feels *you*.

I am interconnected with the whole field. I have so much power just by being here. I can actually play in this field, and this field plays in me. It's not just the Field of Awareness but the Field of Desire, the Field of Eros. It's the Field of Outrageous Love, if you will. And I rest in that field.

That's the True Self, the second answer to *Who are you?*

UNIQUE SELF: I AM A PUZZLE PIECE THAT COMPLETES THE PUZZLE

The problem is that there's a contradiction between these two answers.

The Western Enlightenment says I am a separate self—and realizing that I am not part of a larger field is how I transcend suffering. We established universal human rights by establishing the dignity and centrality of the separate self.

Eastern enlightenment uses the same word, *enlightenment*, but it says the exact opposite is true. What is enlightenment? The realization that I'm *not* a separate self, that I'm one with the field (generally the Field of Awareness). More deeply, more profoundly, it can also mean that I'm one with the Field of Eros, with the Field of Outrageous Love, with the Field of Desire. But I'm one with the field.

So which one is true?

We've begun to understand that we need to bring together these two positions and create an intimacy between them. Instead of these two positions being opposed to each other, we need to hold them together. **We need to move from polarization to paradox and realize that I am** *both* **separate self** *and* **True Self—and that separate self plus True Self** *creates* **something.** If you get that there is actually dignity to separate self, and there is dignity to True Self, you realize the following:

- I am part of the field, but I am also *distinct*—and that distinction is my *uniqueness.*
- In some profound and real sense, I am unique. I have a unique perspective that's unlike any other.
- My separate self is by itself an illusion, but it's pointing to something real: my irreducible uniqueness.

True Self plus my irreducible uniqueness equals my Unique Self.

That's a deeper answer. *Who am I?* I am a Unique Self.

What does it mean to be a Unique Self? I am an irreducible unique expression of the Field of Consciousness, but I'm even more than that.

I am a unique configuration of desire. **If True Self is the entire Field of Desire, then my Unique Self is not just my unique perspective, or my**

unique quality of consciousness, or my unique awareness—it's actually my unique Field of Desire.

My Unique Self is both my particle and my wave, together.

EVOLUTIONARY UNIQUE SELF: I AM A PUZZLE PIECE THAT EVOLVES THE PUZZLE

Then finally, I realize that my Unique Self lives in the context of evolution. It is not just that I am a unique expression of *eternity*. True Self is eternity. True Self is beneath time and space. No, I am more than that, I am *Evolutionary* Unique Self.

As I am living in an evolutionary context, reality is not just *eternity*—it's also *evolution*.

- ◆ It's not just *being*—eternity.
- ◆ It's also *becoming*—the evolutionary impulse.

I am a unique expression of the evolutionary impulse. I am Evolutionary Unique Self.

I am not just Unique Self. I am Evolutionary Unique Self. I am the personal face of the evolutionary impulse.

Let's just recapitulate that again.

As a separate self, I am a puzzle piece. I might be yearning for a larger puzzle, but no, there's no real larger puzzle. I'm just a separate self. Is that crazy-making? Of course it's crazy-making. It causes mental breakdown because I am yearning to be part of this larger puzzle, but the reductive materialism of modernity tells me there is no larger puzzle, I am just a separate self.

It is crazy-making, but it's also partially true. I *am* a separate self. **Separate self is real in the mind of God. It's just not *all* I am.**

Then I move beyond my exclusive identification with separate self. I don't *reject* separate self. Most enlightenment teachings say, *Reject separate self, reject your story.* No, I don't reject my story. I don't reject separate self. **I move beyond *exclusive identification* with separate self.**

I realize I am True Self. True Self means there is no puzzle piece. There is just the one, the puzzle of the one, the one of the puzzle. We get rid of the puzzle pieces. There is just the one puzzle.

The problem with True Self is that when I look closely, I see these little lines between the puzzle pieces. I have this experience of *separateness.* I'm told by my teachers that that experience is an illusion, but I feel that it is real. I am Marc, in some sense. That's also crazy-making. That also causes a mental breakdown in its own way. I cannot deny my story.

I have to resolve those two, and go from the polarity between them to paradox.

I am actually a Unique Self, which means I am a puzzle piece that completes the puzzle around me. But then I realize: *No, it is not just that I fit in and by my very existence, I complete it.*

It's not just that my being completes the puzzle, but my becoming evolves the puzzle.

I am a puzzle piece that evolves the entire puzzle. I'm Evolutionary Unique Self.

Those are the four selves.

This is key. This is the core. Even though we may have heard this before, we settle into it, integrate it. We hear it again. It's just like in a marriage. We don't say, "Oh, I said I love you yesterday, so I don't need to say it today."

We go deep into it. We feel it.

THREE SELVES MODEL

We call the second model of self the Three Selves. The three selves are temporal: the psychological self, the mystical self, and the evolutionary/future self. These two models are actually one.

PSYCHOLOGICAL SELF: DEFINED BY THE PAST

The separate self, in one of its faces, is *the psychological self.*

What's the psychological self? **The psychological self is defined by the past.** All of psychology, as Martin Seligman pointed out, points to yesterday, to the past. In other words, Western psychology realized the past is a key to everything:

- What happened yesterday?
- What's my early childhood?
- What's my trauma?
- What's my relationship to my mother?

When Freud was working with his mentor Josef Breuer in Vienna, there was this large group of women with hysteria, who were dismissed by society as being somehow insane and beyond the pale. Breuer had this realization that maybe they had been abused. Maybe there had been a violation in the past, which is now showing up in the present.

There was this realization that the past is not just gone.

The past lives in the present.

This all concerns my early trauma, my early conditioning, my early culture, my attachment style with my mother or my father. Do I have an *avoidant attachment* style, an *anxious attachment* style, a *disorganized attachment* style? Attachment Theory is a major school of psychology that emerged from John Bowlby, after World War II in a monumental work called *Attachment and Loss,* and was later picked up by Mary Ainsworth in the mid-1960s. And if you want to read a very good book that recapitulates this conversation well, check out *Upheavals of Thought: The Intelligence of Emotions* by Martha Nussbaum.

Psychological self says: *the past rules.*

- The key to unlocking the present is in the past.
- Go back to the past and rework.
- Rework the moment of your birth. Was I wanted or was I not wanted?
- Rework your early childhood.

This is all unimaginably important. One of the great contributions to the evolution of consciousness made by the West is this development of Western psychology, understanding the language of emotions that comes from the past.

The dimension of Reality which rules the separate self is the past. I am defined by the past. Antecedent causation causes almost everything. If you're only a separate self and the past rules everything that you are, then it's only the past that you need to work with in order to unlock the present.

The past, of course, is in some sense causative, in many ways that are invisible to you. The notion that, for example, you have free will is not simple for a psychological separate self, especially if you are a materialist. In other words, **if you are simply the material structure of your body, a separate self defined by the past, then the notion that you would be able to choose would be absurd because everything in the material world is determined by antecedent causation.**

A separate self—in a classical materialist cosmos, or a dualist cosmos in which spirit is *outside* of the world, but the world itself is material—is determined by yesterday.

There is a fantastic movie about this, called *The Adjustment Bureau*. I want to recommend it to everyone. It's about freedom. The assumption is, well, if you are only a separate self in a materialist world, then you are totally defined by yesterday. There is no freedom.

To sum up: the psychological self is an expression of the separate self. What's the primary frame of time that matters for the psychological self and the separate self? The past.

MYSTICAL SELF: THE ETERNAL NOW

We go from psychological self to True Self. And True Self is almost identical to what we call *mystical self*, or the enlightened self. The mystical self says, *Don't worry about the past. Fire your psychologist. That's completely overrated. It's not where you should be. You should focus on the present.* **Step into the eternity that lives in the present**.

The present is not the *here and now* moment. The present is the full presence of eternity, which is beneath space and time. It's Eternal Now. It's always here right now, and it takes you into the Eternal Now. As I am here present now, that opens the door, the portal, into the Eternal Now. That's the mystical self. **The True Self and the mystical self are actually the same.**

If I can actually step into the fullness of the presence, which lives in the present, I will be liberated. While the psychological self says, "I'm liberated by my engagement with the past," the mystical self says, "I'm liberated by engaging with the present."

It's beautiful. So be here now. *The Power of the Now*. God's name is *Now*— *Yod, Hei, Vav, Hei*—the last three letters of God's name refer to now, to the present.

The spiritual practice for the transformation of the separate self and the psychological self is doing psychological work. **Across the Western world, the contemporary spiritual practice has become therapy**. Therapists and psychologists are forms of modern religious practitioners. Like in many spiritual practices—there's not a lot of competent rabbis, priests, ministers,

ANSWERING THE QUESTION, "WHO AM I?"

and imams—there are not that many competent therapists. And the difference between a really good practitioner and an average one is everything.

The practice of liberation for the mystical self is not therapy. It's not psychology. It's some sort of practice that takes you deep into the fullness of the present.

It might be the ecstatic dance movement of whirling dervishes in Sufism.

It might be the Zazen sitting practice of Zen Buddhism.

It might be a chanting practice of Hebrew mysticism that takes me into the fullness of the present.

It might be other kinds of silent practices.

It might be nature practices that take me into the full spaciousness of the Field of Eros and Desire. I can actually feel the field. I might sit and gaze at the ocean. Around the world, people from all walks of life go to gaze at the ocean. It's an intuitive practice, where you can access the fullness of the Field of Eros, of Desire.

This Field of True Self already has in it this quality of *desire*. It's not just constant. **It's being *and* becoming, even at the level of True Self—but it's not that I'm *trying* to become. I am just part of the field.** I am inseparable from the field. It's the realization that I'm part of that field. It's not necessarily that there's something to do there. It's just that I realize my identity as a part of the field.

I am awareness. I am consciousness. I am desire. I am Eros.

I am Outrageous Love.

It's more than *I am that I am*. For the last fifteen years, in teaching and in writing, I've rejected the notion of *I am that I am*. That's a limited version of True Self, only one face of True Self. It's the way it's usually taught, but it's not accurate in terms of realization, in terms of *dharma*. True Self is also:

I am one with the Field of Desire. I am one with the Field of Eros. I am one with the Field of Outrageous Love. I am being *and* I am becoming.

But I am one with the field. I am one with the Force. In *Star Wars*, when they're stealing the plans for the Death Star, one of them keeps saying, "I am one with the Force. I am one with the Force. I am one with the Force." That's True Self.

FUTURE/EVOLUTIONARY SELF: THE CALL OF THE FUTURE

Now it gets very beautiful here—**Unique Self calls the future in**. It's a different moment. Unique Self, by its nature, is also future self. It's very beautiful and it's very deep.

When I am in my Unique Self, I have the experience of being not *just* present and one with the field. I am unique. I am not just one with the Field of Desire—but I have a unique configuration of desire. **My unique configuration of desire is trying to call in a specific future.** There's a future self that enters into my present and calls me forward. Unique Self and Evolutionary Unique Self together are what we call, in the second model, *future self* or *evolutionary self*, which means that the future is now introduced.

> *If psychological self/separate self is the past, and mystical self/true Self is the present, then Unique Self and Evolutionary Unique Self is the call of the future.*

If you look at the four-letter name of God—from right to left—the letters two, three, and four are *Hei, Vav. Hei—hoveh,* which means present. That's mystical self. That's the eternal present.

Yod, the first letter, always represents in Hebrew, *Ehyeh*. It's always the future. It's that which will be. People always quote *I am that I am* from God's conversation with Moses. But of course, that's not what it says. It doesn't say any place, "I am that I am." That's a wrong adaption of it. It actually reads, *Ehyeh. Asher Ehyeh*, "I will be what I will be." It's future. *Ehyeh*, "I will be what I will be." That's the *Yod*. The *Yod* is *Ehyeh*. That's the future.

So, what is the name of God? **The name of God is a conjunction of the future self and the mystical self.**

What's exciting is that we just took these two models of self, which we've done many times—and, for the first time, we put them together. The Four Selves and the Three Selves are actually one model:

- Psychological self is a facet of separate self.
- Mystical self is another way of talking about True Self.
- Future self is a combination of Unique Self and Evolutionary Unique Self.

THE CULTURE IS OPERATING OFF OF A VERY NARROW NOTION OF SELF

All of that is missing from the *Barbie* movie. The only thing that lives in *Barbie* is a materialist desiccated separate self. It's an impoverished story of self, a superficial and shallow answer to the question, *Who am I?* We're lost in the shallows of self. The surface notion of self that informs *Barbie* is the separate self. That's all that's there. Of course, it's not even a *healthy* separate self. It's a broken shadow form of separate self. That's what the *Barbie* movie is based on.

It's unimaginably important to understand that **the entire culture is operating from this very, very narrow notion of self,** which ignores empiricism. It ignores all of the empirical realizations of True Self and mystical self in all of the interior sciences, in all of the great traditions across time.

The realization of True Self and mystical self by the most subtle and speculative minds are completely ignored.

It also ignores all of the evolutionary and complexity sciences—systems theory, complexity theory, chaos theory, evolutionary theory, emergence theory—which demonstrate that the person is part of this larger system. It ignores all expressions of becoming, the realization of the sciences that there is a future that's calling the present into its next phase of emergence— what Whitehead called *the lure of becoming*, or *the allurement of creative emergence*. That's the call of the future.

I just want to you to get how shocking this is. We put a movie into the center of culture, which essentially ignores fundamental aspects of who the person is. It ignores all of the empiricism of True Self (mystical self), located in the classical interior sciences, and it ignores all of the empiricism of evolutionary science, systems theory, complexity theory, chaos theory and sciences—and gives us a desiccated notion of self. That's what *Barbie* does.

The beginning of the response to the meta-crisis is a new answer to the question, Who are you?

This is who we are. This is where we are. This is our location. It's beautiful. This is core, and it's foundational. And if we never, God forbid, met again and you get this, it changes everything.

Remember that as Evolutionary Unique Self, you participate and play your instrument in the Unique Self Symphony. That's what Unique Self Symphony is—when you have a unique instrument to play in the Unique Self Symphony that calls forth this evolving music, that calls forth this evolving symphony, that calls forth the future.

MY DEEPEST HEART'S DESIRE IS THE DESIRE OF EVOLUTION ITSELF

Let's locate this in a prayer formula, which puts it all together.

Who are you?

You are an irreducibly unique expression of the LoveIntelligence, LoveBeauty, and LoveDesire of All-That-Is, that lives *in* you, *as* you, and *through* you, that never was, is, or will be ever again—other than through you.

As such, you have a unique story. You have a unique perspective. You have a unique past.

They come together in your unique present to allow you to give your unique gift to the future, to your unique circle of intimacy and influence that can be given by no one that ever was, is, or will be other than you.

As such, you are the creative evolutionary force of Outrageous Love, of Eros, of Evolutionary Love that stands on the abyss of darkness and says, "Let there be light."

You are a unique configuration of wave and particle. *Particle* is your separate self. *Wave* is you as part of the past, present, and future. **Your wave and particle come together and you form a unique configuration of Eros, intimacy, and desire.** Oh my God! Wow!

And then you have this direct experience: not only do I trust the field, but the field trusts me, and the field needs me. I am held in the timeless time and in the placeless place. And yet, I am the evolutionary impulse itself uniquely incarnate in me, as me, and through me. As such, **my deepest heart's desire is the desire of evolution itself.**

It's from this place that we're going to pray now.

We are going to do a moment of prayer, like we always do every week, with *the holy and the broken Hallelujah*. But can you feel the difference now?

181

I pray one way if I'm only separate self. If I'm only separate self, I throw myself on the Divine and I say, *Help me.* Whether I'm a broken separate self or I'm a dignified separate self, I say, *It's me,* I am here, and God—or whoever I'm talking to—is over there, and I'm saying, *Please help me.* And this is beautiful and true.

But then, as True Self:

- I am in the field with the Divine, part of the Field of Eros.
- I'm part of the Field of Love.
- I'm part of the Field of Evolutionary Love.

It's like one part of the field turning to another part of the field and saying, *I'm part of you. Help me. Hold me.* It's like cells in one part of the body asking cells in the other part of the body to help them flourish and thrive. It's an entirely different conversation. **We're deeply aware of each other, and we feel each other, and we're saying,** *Feel me feeling you as I feel you feeling me.* **It's a prayer of an entirely different intimacy.**

When I pray as Unique Self and Evolutionary Unique Self, I say, *Let me be your partner. Not only do I trust you, but I know that you trust me, and I want to partner with you, and I'm going to give you all I have, and I'm going to literally be your partner, Divine. I'm going to be your partner, Infinite Intimate that knows my name.*

I need all those selves to be together in prayer.

- I pray from separate self, from psychological self.
- I pray from True Self, from mystical self.
- I pray from Unique Self, Evolutionary Self, calling in the future.

Let's step into prayer. Heal the brokenness. Heal the pain. Heal the hurt. Heal the incompleteness. Heal everything that needs being healed.

If I'm praying from True Self and from mystical self, and I feel my fullness with the wider field, I turn to the wider field of life and I say, *Hold me and help me and let me know that I'm with you and let me know that I'm not alone and let me rest in you.*

And if I'm praying from Unique Self and Evolutionary Self, and I know that my deepest heart's desire is the desire of evolution itself, of Divinity herself, I say, *I'm going to partner with you. No matter what, I'm going to cry with you, Divinity. I'm going to cry with you, Infinite, and I'm going to laugh with you, and I'm here to partner with you.*

THERE IS ONE TRUTH

What does this have to do with what's happening in Ukraine right now?

It has to do with everything. This is everything.

This is the shared Field of Value that we all have to be a part of. **We all live together in this Field of Value, in this story of value, which is fact.**

My friend and our board chair at the center, Aubrey Marcus, just went to Jake Paul's fight. He is an influencer fighter now. Aubrey texted me and said that they won the fight, and that when Jake wins a fight, he says, "Facts. Facts." And his whole gang says this. What they mean by *facts* is, "Oh God, we've got to reclaim facts. We've got to reclaim the real. There's something that's real, fact."

Facts, meaning *it's true*. It's true, but we have to reclaim truth, and truth means there is a one truth. One truth is not a dogmatic truth that I impose upon you. There is one truth. There is one goodness, and there is one breath, and there is one love. It means that we're not so fragmented; we actually experience that we're all unique instruments of one music, and that music is a story.

---

*There is a shared Story of Value, and that
which unites us is so much greater than that
which divides us. It's only a shared truth that
can respond to the meta-crisis.*

What we need to do is—if we want Torah, a new *dharma* to come forth
from Zion—we need to tell the new Story of Value.

Holiness doesn't live in a particular piece of ground by itself. That piece of
ground has to be a ground of Value. The single most vital moral imperative
for Israel and Gaza, and for Russia and Ukraine, is to demand that everyone
do the deep work.

But we cannot just *demand* it. We have to actually do the deep work
ourselves, and write it up, and write a Great Library, and tell a story that's
translated in all languages. Right now, if I had to give a book to leading
Russian intellectuals and say, "This is a good Story of Value that you can
actually rest in," I do not know. I don't have a book to give anyone. That's
why we wrote a book called *First Principles & First Values*—and we're just
beginning. There are little fragments here and fragments there. We don't
have a Great Library yet.

We stopped writing as a culture. We exploded in the progress of exteriors,
and we stopped evolving in our interiors, and the gap between interiors
and exteriors widened and widened, and we created exponential ways to
destroy ourselves without developing commensurate exponential wisdom
to allow us to use and deploy those technologies.

That's what we're doing. **The most activist thing we can do to respond
to the meta-crisis is to begin to create a coherence in the world, to
move from polarization to paradox.** We each have unique and distinct

instruments in the symphony. We're all playing music, and the story that we're telling now is our music. We all bring our holy and broken *Hallelujahs*.

Every nation, every people, every person, every religion, every country has:

- Its version of separate self (win/lose metrics)
- Its True Self, its own deep mystical truth
- Its Unique Self, its unique gift
- Its Evolutionary Unique Self, its contribution to evolution

All the four selves live not just in a person. They also live in collectives. And then we come together, and we become a Unique Self Symphony.

Oh my God! That's worth being alive for.

Let's take us inside, into prayer, into the holy and the broken *Hallelujah*.

CHAPTER THIRTEEN

THE DIVINE DELIGHT AND DEVASTATION OF DEVOTION AND HER DIGNITIES: VISIONS OF UNIQUE SELF AND UNIQUE SELF SYMPHONY

Episode 381 — February 11, 2024

YOU CANNOT LIVE IN JOY WITHOUT BEING IN DEVOTION

Welcome, everyone! *Cha!*

Cha means the aliveness that words can't capture. That's *cha*. It's the poignancy, it's the potency, it's the fullness of life that words can't capture.

And when you really want to say *cha*, you say *giga-cha*.

I have a dear friend who I text with every day. We text, back and forth, the levels of *cha*.

Is it a *giga-cha* day? Is it a *mega-cha* day? Is it a *regular cha* day?

Cha is like *yes! Yes! Yes! Yes! Yes!*

And this *Yes* is not a bypass. It's not an override of the pain. It is not superficial, or flaccid, or insipid. *Cha* is *Yes*. It is the resounding, unrelenting commitment to the fullness and goodness of this moment right now, in this very second.

So welcome, everyone.

We have a huge, wildly important topic today—**devotion**.

How can you be fiercely independent, wildly autonomous, and radically devoted?

That's the question. **You actually cannot live in joy—*I* cannot live in joy, *we* cannot live in joy—without being in mad devotion.**

Devotion has its distortions, so it requires discernment. We need *distinctions* around devotion, but before we get to the distinctions, I want to just *invoke* devotion.

We often dismiss devotion. Devotion is that which someone does when they're not successful.

- We say about a man who is not successful, "But he's a very devoted husband, he's a devoted father."
- About a woman who doesn't meet society's standards of whatever society is expecting from her—whether in terms of success or beauty and all of the expectations of a superficial society that hasn't yet found its heart and soul, that hasn't yet burst into *Homo amor*—we say about the woman, "Yeah, but she's a very devoted mother, or wife."

There is something dark about devotion. You are somehow lost. **Devotion is understood, in some sense, to be in opposition to dignity.** And in modern therapeutic terms, devotion is connected to codependency, which is the ultimate sin.

We need to find our way to devotion that's whole and powerful. Because—again—you cannot be in joy without devotion. Can't be done. No joy without devotion.

- Step one, Reality is desire.
- Step two, desire is about devotion. My desire means there is something that's not yet here and I want it—but I'm actually devoted, in some sense, to realizing it.

But it's more than that. It's deeper. That's level one of desire and devotion.

Desire is a quality of the wider Field of Eros. Desire lives across all fields of Reality. Reality is Desire, and sexuality models Eros.

- The sexual models the erotic; it doesn't exhaust the erotic.
- Sexual desire models desire; it doesn't exhaust desire.

When you are in desire, what is desire arousing in you? What is the characteristic of desire? **The characteristic of desire is devotion**. Whenever you are on your knees, you are always on your knees to God. It's an act of devotion. It's a *servicing of*, it's a *devotion to*. There is an unimaginable quality of devotion in desire, in lovemaking.

Devotion and desire are fundamentally related to each other. And we're going to understand powerfully that **devotion is an expression of *Homo amor*—and *Homo amor* is Unique Self and Unique Self Symphony**.

- There is no devotion that's whole outside of the context of Unique Self.
- There is no devotion that's whole outside of the context of Unique Self Symphony.

We need to get to a devotion that's whole, and powerful, and potent—and we need to avoid the pathology of devotion.

But first, we need to take devotion back. Devotion is not a pathology *per se*. **Devotion is the mad, gorgeous power of Cosmos**. The very quality of Divinity, the very quality of the Infinite, is the Infinite Intimate—and the Infinite is in *devotion* to the finite.

The name of God is the Infinite Intimate.
The Infinite is in devotion to finitude.

That's the paradox of the Infinite: the Infinite is all-powerful, radically alive, not in need—in any classical sense at least—of the finitude of the manifest world. And yet, the name of God is the Infinite Intimate. **The Infinite is in devotion to her intimates.** Wow!

ANNA AKHMATOVA AS A SYMBOL OF DEVOTION: WHERE CATASTROPHE LED THEM, I WAS THERE

Let's just *feel* this devotion.

I want to share with you something personal, something intimate that I was thinking about early this morning. I went to do my doctorate, essentially, so my mother would be happy. Jewish mothers, sons, academic degrees—you know how that all works. I went to Oxford so my mother could tell people, "Oh, my son, he's in Oxford and he's getting a doctorate." I got some points with mom there. That was good.

When I was in Oxford, I was in the college that had the library of Isaiah Berlin. He was one of the most fascinating and brilliant figures in contemporary philosophy, one of the great dons of Oxford, one of the great philosophers of the twentieth century. He was also very involved in politics. I was in the library in Oxford, surrounded by Isaiah Berlin's books. And they're crazy interesting and beautiful.

I happened across a book about how Isaiah Berlin went to Russia. It's 1945, he was working for the British government, he goes to Russia, and he wants to meet with a poet whose name is Anna Akhmatova. They tell him that she is still alive, and so he goes to meet her. They have this mad night together—not a night of sexing, but a night of Eros. They fall madly in love with each other, I would say. It is this incredible meeting, which took place in Leningrad.

Let's understand who Anna Akhmatova was, and the context.

The way the West tells the story of World War II, it's the Allies who defeated Nazism. But for many years, they skipped over the incredible and unimaginable suffering of the Russian people and the Russian army, which was essential in defeating Nazism—an unimaginable story of suffering, heroism, and bravery. It was only after the Cold War thawed that there was some beginning of a realization of what the devotion of Russia was.

Russia was devotion. Russia literally *became* devotion.

Anna Akhmatova's probably greatest poem is called "Requiem," and it opens with these four lines:

> Unmoved by the glamor of alien skies,
> By asylum in faraway cities, I
> Chose to remain with my people: where
> Catastrophe led them, I was there.

She tells many stories, but included in them was her own suffering trying to protect her family in Leningrad. She writes:

> In the terrible years of the Yezhov terror, I spent seventeen months queuing outside the prisons of Leningrad.

Just to get a little bit of her story, her first husband was executed by the secret police in 1921. Her third husband and her son spent many years in the gulag. And she would wait, freezing in these very long lines, trying to deal with an impossible gulag bureaucracy—trying to somehow protect them, trying somehow to help them.

I just want you to get the image of devotion. This woman who's been outside the prisons of Leningrad for seventeen months all day, all day from the beginning to the end, in line. Almost like in Kafka's trial, these impossible lines in impossible contexts.

Then she writes:

> On one occasion someone recognized me. It was a woman
> who was standing near me in the queue, with lips of a bluish
> color, and then, waking from that state of numbness which was
> characteristic of us all, she quietly asked me (for everyone spoke
> in a whisper in those days): "And can you write about this?"
> And I replied, "I can." And then something like a smile flickered
> across what was once her face.

I've looked at the lines of "Requiem," which are about suffering. They are
about the horror of Stalin, all mixed up with all of the brutality of this impossible hidden time.

**She is in devotion, she's for seventeen months in queue. Her devotion is
to her son and to her husband, but her devotion is also to the writing.**

- ◆ She is going to write, and she is writing in devotion.
- ◆ She is not writing because she is going to get published
  tomorrow.
- ◆ She is in devotion to Goodness itself.
- ◆ She is in devotion to Truth.
- ◆ She is in devotion to Beauty.
- ◆ She is in devotion to the Word.

She has this trust that her devotion to the Word has dignity, and ultimately
will bear fruit.

I came across her just sitting there, while I was writing about Aramaic texts
all night and all day. I wrote the doctorate surrounded by Isaiah Berlin's
books—and he met her in 1945 and spent a night with her—a night of
radical Eros in which Berlin is young and naive, and she is older and wiser.
And yet, this impossible meeting takes place.

For me, she has always been a symbol of devotion.

I want to begin with that kind of devotion. We'll get to the later stages of devotion, but I just want you to feel devotion with that image. I want to just invoke devotion with you.

EVOLUTIONARY LOVE CODE: THE EVOLUTION OF DESIRE IS THE EVOLUTION OF DEVOTION

Reality is desire.

Desire is devotion.

Devotion is the placing of attention.

Homo amor is devoted, but the devotion of *Homo amor* is fundamentally different from the devotion of *Homo sapiens*. Devotion shows up in one way in the premodern period, then there is the devotion of modernity, which is followed by postmodernity's deconstruction of devotion.

The new Story of Value—CosmoErotic Humanism—reclaims devotion at a higher level of consciousness.

Devotion shows up differently as separate self, as True Self, as Unique Self, as Evolutionary Unique Self, and in Unique Self Symphony.

Devotion shows up differently at each of the three stations of love.

Indeed, evolution is the evolution of desire. The evolution of desire is the evolution of devotion, the evolution of devotion is the evolution of love, and the evolution of love is the birth of *Homo amor*.

DEVOTION IS AN EXPRESSION OF THE DEPTH OF DESIRE

We are going to hear, just for three minutes, Sally Kempton. The great teacher Sally Kempton, Swami Durgananda, a powerful feminist, a powerful voice against abuse, and a powerful voice for the dignity of the feminine. Sally writes and talks about devotion. Let's hear an incredible little piece from Sally Kempton, our dear, dear friend and one of the powerful women who stood with the Center for so many years.

This clip is called "My Life of Devotion."

If anything characterizes *Homo amor*, it's devotion.

The first quick move we can make is: I am devoted to *myself*. I get that, and that's important. As I said earlier, true devotion lives in the context of Unique Self. Sally's life was a journey towards that realization, and Sally and I spent many hours deepening this Unique Self realization together.

First, let's first *claim* devotion. Let's claim devotion and not be afraid of devotion.

Devotee is a word that we today associate with the cult, with pre-personal, abusive cults. That's where you are a devotee. That's tragic and not true. Of course, you can pathologize devotion. Of course, there are degraded forms of devotion, but that's not what true devotion *is*.

Devotion is stunning.

My life is devotion, and I am in devotion.

I'm in deep devotion to *She*, in devotion to our mission, in devotion to the community, and in devotion to individuals in the community.

It's not "I'm *committed* to." It's "I'm *in devotion* to." I want to feel that quality.

Devotion is not in contradiction to autonomy. It's not in contradiction to my fierce sense of irreducible uniqueness, nor should it be in contradiction to your fierce sense of irreducible uniqueness.

What is the quality of devotion? Devotion is an expression of the depth of my desire—the more I desire, the more I'm devoted.

- The more I desire to be in union with the Good, the more I'm devoted to the Good.

- The more I desire to be in union with She, the more I'm devoted to She.
- The more I desire to be in union with the True, the more devoted I am to the True.

For example, I once read a beautiful set of paragraphs written by Steven Weinberg on muons, these subatomic particles. It was clear that Weinberg was in devotion to muons—the radical devotion of the scientist to Truth, to the quality of Truth.

It's devotion to Beauty—but not Beauty as a tinsel Beauty, not Beauty as pseudo-eros. It's but devotion to Eros itself, to the Beauty that includes all contradictions.

I remember my friend Mori, a woman I was madly in love with. We lived together in the same house, in separate apartments. We had dinner together every Friday night, but we never had any physical contact. When I met her, I was about thirty-one, and she must have been eighty or eighty-five. She was this very old Moroccan or Yemenite woman who had come to Israel when the state was founded. Her children had abandoned her, and we happened to be living in adjoining apartments. Her wrinkled face was the most beautiful face you could imagine.

I was in devotion to Mori.

Devotion means I show up no matter what.

- I arouse myself out of my torporific slumber.
- I find my aliveness.
- I place my aliveness on the altar of She for the sake of a greater wholeness, for the sake of manifesting the most beautiful, good, and true world that we've always known is possible.

The pure joy of devotion, the trembling aliveness of devotion, the showing up—let's just feel into that quality of devotion, and the mad delight.

There is a *steadiness* to it. I show up even when I don't really feel like it. It's consistent.

When someone experiences devotion, when someone in relationship to you is in devotion, you can rest in that devotion.

Just from my perspective, I'm devoted to people, and they know they can rest in my devotion. As long as I'm alive, I will try and show up, and be committed forever in mad devotion. Even when it doesn't make sense, and when it's politically inappropriate, and it economically borders on ruinous—we are devoted. We show up.

When you eat, you can taste food that was prepared in devotion. You can taste food that was prepared efficiently—or the food that's prepared in devotion. We are in devotion to each other. **We are devotional beings.**

Yes, I need to be discerning about where—on what altars—to place my devotion. Yes, that's all true. Because after all, isn't *jihad* a false devotion? Of course, it is. So **we're going to need to make distinctions around devotion.**

But first, my friends, let's breathe in that quality of devotion. Devotion means we keep our commitments. We keep our word in the best way we can, if we don't, we notice it, then we recommit. That's devotion.

DEVOTION IN PREMODERNITY, MODERNITY, AND POSTMODERNITY

Let's go deeper and look at premodern devotion, modern devotion, and postmodern devotion.

Premodern devotion is generally devotion to a religion—a religion in which there's a god or a religious authority at the center.

At its best, we're fulfilled through our devotion. But often it meant giving ourselves up. It meant an abnegation of self. It meant a degradation of self. In the best situations, it didn't. But for the masses, devotion was part of the unfulfilled realization of the human potentiality of a fully dignified self, independent of what were often superficial and misplaced devotions.

Devotion was a beautiful quality of premodernity, but also a quality that was often pathological because the self wasn't realized.

Anthony Storr is a very good psychoanalyst and a very good thinker. He wrote a book called *Solitude*, and there's a section where he traces the word *self*. It first appeared in the dictionary in the Renaissance.

To have real devotion, I first need to be a self.

Devotion to king, to country, to kingdom, to empire—those are the loci of premodern devotion. Or devotion to a god who is dissociated from, or at least separate from, Reality. God is outside of Reality, and I am in devotion to that external god.

That's not entirely wrong—it's just limited.

You've got to begin with understanding that this premodern notion of devotion wasn't just a deception. It was also speaking to a very deep realization, deep inside the Anthro-Ontology of the human being, in the human knowing of the nature of existence—**the realization that we are in devotion**.

In the text of the Western canon called *Genesis*, you have Adam and Eve, who are archetypal, mythic figures, and then you have Cain and Abel, who go to offer sacrifice. In sacrifice, I'm offering something up, I'm in devotion. If you read the text, you notice that there's no *command* to sacrifice. Why are they *offering* sacrifice? No one asked them for a sacrifice.

The impulse to devotion lives deep inside.

The word for sacrifice in the original Hebrew is *korban*. It means intimate closeness and sacrifice, intimacy and sacrifice, because there is no intimacy without sacrifice. **There is no intimacy without devotion**. You can't be intimate without being devoted.

In modernity, the locus of devotion shifted to the physical world, and to the knowing of the nature of the physical world. It is a new form of devotion.

We shift to measurement, which is a desire to know, to understand. There is a devotion to Truth. I don't want dogma of premodernity—I want to know the Truth.

Science is animated by the Eros of this new devotion to facts—to the stories of science, the factual stories of science.

There is also a devotion to my own interiors called psychology. I want to go inside myself and know what's going on inside of me.

That's the devotion of modernity.

Postmodernity completely *deconstructs* devotion, because postmodernity says there are no stories that are true. There are no values that are real. They are all socially constructed. There is no essence to be devoted *to*. What I used to be in devotion to is really an ephemeral myth, a figment of my imagination, a social construct, a fiction. Those are the words used by postmodernity.

Postmodernity says, deconstruct your devotions. Your devotions are degraded. Therefore, says postmodernity, *your devotion must be some power move someone is making*. You're naive. Someone is taking advantage of you. They're exerting power over you by demanding your devotion. If you would actually grow up, mature, and go to therapy, you would actually liberate yourself from these degraded devotions.

That's postmodernity. **Postmodernity deconstructs devotion.**

WE NEED TO DECONSTRUCT DEVOTION IN ORDER TO RESURRECT IT

We need to go post-postmodernity. The breakdown of devotion has led to the meta-crisis. Opposite to devotion are the generator functions of the meta-crisis:

1. Rivalrous conflict governed by win/lose metrics, which is the polar opposite of devotion—anyone who is devoted is considered a fool.
2. Rivalrous conflict governed by win/lose metrics, which governs all of the relationships in society—economic, political, social, psychological, technological—then generates fragile, complicated systems.

A complicated system means that the system is fragile. It can break down. It's optimized for efficiency, not resiliency, because **there can only be resiliency if there is devotion. The parts have to know each other—they have to be in devotion to each other.**

When a financial instrument ripples through the world markets wreaking destruction, it's because the people who created it are non-intimate with the broader swaths of Reality that they are impacting. They are operating based on a rivalrous conflict governed by win/lose metrics. There is no devotion. Those are the generator functions for the meta-crisis, and underneath both of them is a collapse of intimacy.

Intimacy arouses devotion. The meta-crisis is an expression of a crisis of devotion.

There's a reason for the crisis: devotion got pathologized. Devotion got hijacked, both in premodernity and in the success stories of modernity,

198

where I am devoted to science and to my inner psychology, and devotion became pseudo-erotic:

+ I am devoted to success.
+ I am devoted to my own emergence for its own sake.

It's a separate-self devotion, which has a bad fragrance. I become egoic, not in a *healthy ego* sense—the ego that differentiates and that has its own sense of parameters and boundaries. Rather, I am in service to one thing only—to my status, to my power, to my superficial expression, not to my authentic expression. I become devoted in a pathological way.

We need to reclaim devotion.

Postmodernity comes along, and it deconstructs the absurdity of the personal devotion of the success story. It also deconstructs the systemic devotions of kingdoms, and religions, and philosophies, and ideologies.

Postmodernity is important. That's why I consistently disagree with my colleague Jordan Peterson, who mocks postmodernity.

No, we *need* to deconstruct devotion. **We need to deconstruct devotion in order to then resurrect devotion at a higher level of consciousness.**

DEVOTION IS THE PLACING OF ATTENTION

The nature of devotion is the placing of attention. When I am devoted to you, I fully place my attention on you. Devotion is a quality of love, it is a quality of Eros. **The nature of Eros, the nature of love, is the placing of attention.** That's why the sexual models the erotic—because the essence of the sexual is the placing of attention. In the sexual, I place my attention. That's why we are excited by the sexual.

The hijacking of the sexual—the movement from the *erotic* universe to the *pornographic* universe—is the movement from Eros to pseudo-eros. Our attention has been hijacked. **The pornographic universe—whether it's**

in sexuality or social media—is hijacking my attention, which deconstructs my capacity for devotion.

The reason social media demarcates the postmodern world is because it has deconstructed devotion and *attention*. In the postmodern world, there is nothing to place attention on.

- In the premodern world, we place attention on the Divine.
- In the modern world, we place attention on psychology and science, on the inner workings of the factual realities.
- The postmodern world says there is no Field of Value, so there's nothing to place attention on. Devotion expresses itself in attention, but postmodernity says there's nothing to be devoted to, and nothing to place your attention on.

The exteriorization of the interior experience of the postmodern mind is the internet, where there's a constant interruption of attention. Attention is constantly being hijacked, constantly being stolen. **The internet is the structure designed for the scattering of attention—but if you scatter attention, you can't be in devotion.** You can't be in devotion to truth, goodness, or beauty.

This is why people jump from teacher to teacher, from project to project, from cause to cause, from book to book—because we can't actually *stay*. We can't focus. We can't stay inside.

One of the things we say to each other when we start a real process of being together—let's say in *Holy of Holies*—is *we are here forever*.

We are here forever. As long as you'll be here, I'll be here. We are here forever, together.

Whatever that means—and of course, *forever* means *you* can leave whenever you want. Anyone who wants to leave can leave whenever they want, but *I* am here forever. We are in devotion. I am in devotion. You choose your devotion—but there is a *forever* quality. You can step in, step out in different ways, but if you're really inside, there is a fundamental *forever* quality.

Whenever devotion is placed, there has to be a forever relationship.

By the way, I've written a lot about sexuality, so people assume I have a liberal position on sexuality. I do not. I don't think there should be sexuality in the world unless there is some sort of forever commitment. That forever commitment might not be marriage, but sexuality is not casual. The second I'm devoted to you, and I've placed my attention on you, that means there should be a connection of some kind between us forever.

I WANT TO PLACE MY ATTENTION ON MY ALLUREMENT

Now, let's resurrect devotion. Let's evolve devotion.

Devotion is a quality of *Homo amor*. What is the realization of *Homo amor*?

I am not just separate self, and my devotion is not just a psychological devotion of separate self, which is very easy to hijack, and distort, and manipulate in abusive ways.

I go from separate self to *True Self*. The devotion of True Self is the realization that we live in the field together. There is **a devotion to the field itself**. It is a devotion to awareness, to the realization of my true nature as awareness.

In the devotion of True Self, I place my attention on my awareness.

I place my attention on consciousness, and I realize that my true nature— *Tat Tvam Asi*, thou art that—is consciousness. That's the quality of True Self.

201

It's beautiful. I am in devotion to the field of consciousness, but that's just the first step of resurrecting devotion. If you stop there, devotion wilts and dies.

Because we are *more* than conscious. **Consciousness is *the beginning* of the inside, but it's not *the Inside of the Inside.***

There is *Sat, Chit,* and *Ananda*—terms from Kashmir Shaivism, from Hinduism:

- *Sat* is being and *Chit* is consciousness, so the inside of *Sat* is *Chit*. The inside of being is consciousness.
- Then, the inside of *Chit* is *Ananda*, and *Ananda* is the play of allurement, the play of desire and intimacy.

So I don't just want to place my attention on awareness.

I want to place my attention on *allurement.*

That's the move from True Self to Unique Self. This is not a regressive move. I'm not moving backwards to separate self.

Separate self is level one.

Level two, I have a healthy separate self which I've now transcended—I ended the trance of being separate, the optical delusion of consciousness, which is the thinking that I'm separate. I realize I am True Self, the singular that has no plural, that I'm not separate from the Field of Consciousness and Awareness.

And then I realize—level three—that I'm actually an irreducible, unique expression of that Field of Consciousness, and that Field of Consciousness is not just a Field of Consciousness. It's also a Field of Desire, Intimacy, and Allurement.

So I place my attention on—I am in devotion to—my allurement because I realize that my Unique Self is my unique set of allurements. And I *clarify* my allurement.

What the internet does is distracts you from your allurement. You can't get allured.

You can't find your way into your allurement.

You can't find your way into your desire.

You're constantly distracted.

You have to place your attention on your desire.

Desire and devotion are inextricably related, so I have to place my attention and be in devotion in order to know who I am. I *do* need devotion to myself, but not devotion to me as a *separate self*. **I am in devotion to my Unique Self, and my Unique Self doesn't separate me from the whole.**

Unique Self is not the coin of alienation, or the coin of separation.

Unique Self is the currency of connection.

Unique Self is the electricity of allurement.

Unique Self is the highway of desire. It's the pathway of desire.

I need to be in devotion to my unique set of allurements, and my allurements allure me to you.

My allurements allure me to that which is not merely my separate self, but to you, to *She*, to communion, with my community, with my teacher, with my family, with my beloveds, and with the larger field.

Homo amor is in communion with the larger whole.

I don't just feel my local community—I feel the whole. *Homo amor* is omni-allured to the whole. Therefore, *Homo amor* is omni-responsible for the whole. Therefore, *Homo amor* is devoted to the whole.

I have a devotion to the whole, which means, **at a moment of meta-crisis, when I have an experience that the whole is breaking down, then I need to find a way to be in service and devotion to the whole.** And if we come together and realize that only a new story changes the vector of the whole, we then become devoted—radically devoted—to enacting this new Story of Value for the sake of the whole, in mad devotion.

That's an example of a Unique Self in devotion, but I'm not doing it *myself*. We're *all together* in devotion to that vision, and we each have a unique instrument to play in the Unique Self Symphony of that vision of allurement.

Devotion means I move from being separate. I'm not separate self but Unique Self. Uniqueness is the currency of connection. Uniqueness means I have a unique piece of music to play.

DEVOTION BEYOND UNIQUE SELF

Widening my field, looking at the whole, feeling the whole, allowing myself to take in the whole—it's beautiful. If I try and embrace much *more* of the whole, I move out of my specialization to take in the whole, and I become a generalist. In that sense, I *spread my attention around* and embrace the whole. That's beautiful.

The scattering of attention is something else. It's not a decision I made, but one that was made for me. I jumped from thing to thing, and I never actually placed my attention with any level of depth.

On the one hand, I want to expand my attention, expand my devotion, and embrace the whole—I want to almost *swallow* the whole.

And yet I want to—not *scatter* but *specialize*.

I want to go *deep*. I want to read every word that Tolstoy ever wrote, and I want to paint a painting for every one of Shakespeare's Sonnets. And from that place of depth, from that devotion to my unique set of allurements, I'll become an artist.

I'll create this new, unique artistry in contributing to the Great Library.

I'll tell a story.

My devotion might be, *I'm going to do this particular piece, for example, of the Great Library that no one else can do.* Perhaps I say, *I'm going to sharpen it, and make it noble and beautiful.* I'll do a piece, and Elena will do a piece, and Ken Wilber will do a piece, and Zohar will do a piece. In other words, we're going to come together. And Krista will do a piece, and Jamie will do a piece, and Jacqueline will do a piece, and Kristina Amelong will do a piece, and then Chahat will do a piece, and Claire is going to do a piece. And of course, Dr. Kincaid is going to run the entire phenomenology section.

Wow! That's my allurement. I'm going to do that. We're going to do that *together.*

We always need to come back to devotion. We need to reclaim devotion—devotion to *She,* to the Field of Eros as it lives in me.

Devotion beyond my egoic and separate self. **Sometimes devotion is even somewhat beyond my Unique Self.** Sometimes, I need to evaluate where we are at this moment in time, and what my unique contribution has to be at this moment in time.

When Israel was first established, the land was filled with malaria, and you had expert doctors and philosophers coming over from Europe, and they became farmers. They became farmers because they were devoted to this vision, and that vision required something. It's beautiful.

I have a friend whose name I can't say. He's a brilliant doctor from Gaza, and he was offered major fellowships in Western universities, but he returned home, knowing full well the horror of Hamas that was oppressing Gazans. He returned in order to take a job at a local medical clinic in a particular place in Gaza because that was his devotion. He let go of a certain dimension of Unique Self.

I often ask, "what's my Unique Self?" I actually want to write philosophical poetry about laughter, and philosophical poetry about all sorts of dimensions of the human experience.

But there is a meta-crisis. And what do we need to do in a meta-crisis?

- Take everything we have.
- Come together in devotion to the whole.
- Articulate, write, and share the new Story of Value.
- Be together in Unique Self Symphony.
- Be in devotion to each other.

The musicians are in devotion to each other.

My Unique Self has to meet both my unique needs and the unique needs of the moment. And of course, the Story of Value would benefit enormously by the poetry of laughter, and by the poetry of tears. Somehow it all comes together in the paradox. When we hold it all together, when we weave it all together, we get wonder and paradox—and we don't get polarity.

What a crazy pleasure, my friends!

What a crazy delight it is to be together!

I'M YOUR MAN

We're going to step into prayer now. Leonard Cohen has a song called "I'm Your Man." He's talking to the feminine, and he's saying, "I'll be anything you want me to be." Let's play that as our prayer.

But first I want to tell you what the song's about. He's playing with sexuality. He's saying, "I'll be this for you and I'll be that to you." There is one video of Leonard Cohen doing that song, and he's like seventy-five years old, maybe closer to 80, and he's wearing a pinstripe double-breasted suit with a hat. You can feel his devotion. This is the reason the song is not felt to be offensive to the feminine: the feminine feels he is in devotion. "I'm your man. I'll be anything you want me to be. I'm in devotion to you."

That's how we turn to *She*.

We turn to *She* and we say, "I'm your man."

When Anna Akhmatova falls in love with Isaiah Berlin that night in Leningrad, they didn't engage in formal sexuality. It was Eros.

They fell in love.

They saw each other.

They recognized each other.

"I'm Your Man" is the song we sing, what we chant in devotion to *She*. It's the chant of devotion. I'm your man, I'm your woman.

INDEX

Volume 22 — Homo Amor and Unique Self

List of Episodes

www.ingramcontent.com/pod-product-compliance
Lightning Source LLC
LaVergne TN
LVHW011151080426
835508LV00007B/345